INVESTING 101

how to invest your way to retiring a millionaire before the age of 65 with a safe, simplified and effective investing and money management system

by Matthew S. Barnes

www.MatthewBarnes-101.com

DISCLAIMER

The information contained in this book is for general information purposes only. Any reliance you place on such information as listed in this book is strictly at your own risk. The author or publisher of this book will not be held liable for any loss or damage including without limitation indirect or consequential loss or damage, or any loss or damage whatsoever arising from loss of data or profits arising out of or in connection with the use of information in this book or the websites it mentions. We have no control over the nature, content and availability of other sites. The inclusion of any links does not necessarily imply recommendation or endorse the views expressed within them. Every effort is made to keep our website up and running smoothly. However, we take no responsibility for, and will not be reliable for, the website being temporarily unavailable due to technical issues beyond our control. There is inherent risk in investing. Past performance does not guarantee future results.

INSIDE THIS LITTLE BOOK IS A SOLID INVESTING SYSTEM THAT CAN WORK FOR YOU WITHOUT YEARS OF MARKET STUDY:

I have been forced to manage my own money for years. In addition to creating a unique way of approaching money management, I also believe I have found a simplified investing approach that has allowed me to make good returns without having to have a PhD in stock market lingo, or rely on financial advisors. I have also been lucky enough to stumble upon an investing niche that has turned out to be a godsend for accelerating returns.

This book is a no-nonsense, practical guide designed for the regular everyday person. It is simple, direct and to the point. You won't find the fluff and excessive wording found in most books.
The system I teach takes very little time and is definitely unique.

Please note that I call my system Investing 101 not because it is a beginners guide to all the technical words and inner workings of the market. I call my system Investing 101 because it is a very simple system that can help you invest very successfully, in only minutes per week, without having to have a collegiate level understanding of every aspect of the market.

Also note that my system goes a bit against the grain- if you are looking for the same old advice that gives you the same old results, this book is not for you.

ACKNOWLEDGMENTS

I'd like to thank my wife, as usual, for putting up with me, and all my errors, while I was learning this system. I can get obsessive over learning sometimes, but she's been by my side through it all.

I'd like to thank Alisha for all the work she has put into this project, as well as all my other ventures- you are a real trooper and a great friend.

I'd also like to acknowledge Robert Kiyosaki, Ken Roberts, Ted Warren, Warren Buffett, Burton H. Pugh, Dave Ramsey and all the other non-conventional money thinkers and traders out there who had the fortitude to buck the accepted way of doing everything and make a new path. I understand the rarity of such a thing, and truly appreciate what you have been able to do.

Lastly I'd like to thank Ken Roberts again, this time for pointing out that investing is as much emotional as it is mental. Mr. Roberts consistently recommended reading books on developing a calm, mental fortitude and not only on the technical aspects of training. I'd like to suggest the same to you. Enhance your ability to invest by not only learning the strategies of investing, but also by studying the workings of the mind. You need the calm of a samurai when the markets start to buck and roll.

CONTENTS

INTRODUCTION

I want to be free of the tyranny of money. I want to be free to do whatever I want to do, and still have enough money to survive. I hate being at the whim of money. I want to simply live, and not have to worry about money. Spiritual issues aside, money controls us, one and all. And I don't like it one bit.

I have been told that when writing a book like this that I need to elaborate, that readers like a story. Getting right to the point, and just listing the bare bones information needed evidently doesn't engage readers enough. My problem is that I want this book to be short and sweet and to the point. I want to tell you, as briefly as possible, what this system is all about and how to do it. I want you to be able to read it quickly, refer to it often and apply it immediately if you would like. I don't want this book to be so long and convoluted that it takes you five years to read, and then when you get done you can't figure out exactly what the system is all about and how to make it work.

As a result, I am going to try and compromise. I am going to tell you more about my story and some of the background than I feel the book needs, but still try to keep it brief and to the point.

I believe that money is freedom- at least with how our world works currently. I hope that this book will help you to reach that freedom. Freedom from the tyranny of money, freedom to do what you want to do, and freedom to be what you want to be, without having to worry about money.

I also want to give you the know how to help others escape the tyranny of money if you would like.

Since you have purchased my book, you can go to the website I have set up to offer more help on this subject and enter the members area.

The website is www.MatthewBarnes-101.com. The members only area has video tutorials and spreadsheets you can use at no charge. The members only password for this first book is QUAN.

I also offer a weekly investing newsletter for those of you that are interested. The members area is free, signing up on my email list is free, but I do charge for the newsletter. You can find all of this on my website.

THE OUTLINE

Let's jump right in and give you the basic outline, the basic gameplan, of my system- it consists of two investment funds:

1) The first thing we are going to do is to figure out how much money you want to retire on comfortably, and at what age you want to try and retire.

   Using a free online calculator, we will estimate how much we need to put away into safe, conservative investments each month in order to hit that retirement goal.

   We will pay that amount each and every week or month into our investment portfolio like it is a bill.

2) Next, we will use an easy formula to calculate how much money you have in excess of your bills.

   That excess money will be split between Fun Money and money that you will use to pay off your debt.

3) Once your debt is paid off, the money you had been using to pay off your debt will be put into a much more aggressive investment fund.

Let me re-emphasize the fact that you will have two investment funds. The first will be very safe and conservative, the second will be much more aggressive.

The first fund will be used to try and secure your retirement. This is where most of your investing will take place.

The second fund, made up of money in excess of your living expenses, will be invested much more aggressively.

This fund makes up a smaller percentage of your overall investments, but it gives you the chance to "swing for the fences".

The second fund is your adventurous fund, where you try to speed up how fast you get to your retirement and how much you end up with. It is a much more aggressive fund.

The overall goal of this system is to create and live off your very own money tree. You put money in, grow that money, and eventually live off the children created by the money you put in. In the end, you will hopefully leave that money tree to your kids when you are gone.

People that grew up without money tend to look at money differently than people who have had money their entire lives. People not used to money tend to spend money as they make it. They buy things like cars and houses. They even spend more than they make by buying on credit.

The rich do it differently. They take the money they earn and instead of spending it once, find a way to live off of it forever. They buy things like rent houses, other real estate, and invest it in the market. In this way, they live off the returns on their money but never touch the actual principle. They make money once and live off of it forever.

Those not used to money do the exact opposite. They spend what they make, and then some usually.

I want to show you how to make money once, but spend it forever.

I will also show you how to protect your money from predators.

Let's get started.

I'M NO EXPERT

The first thing I want to make clear in this little book is that I am no expert. At all. I have no financial degrees; I have no license to be a broker or financial advisor or anything even close to any of that. I am simply a man that got fed up with having other people manage his money.

If you are the type of person that is only interested in information coming from someone with a long list of degrees after their name, I'm not the person for you. If you are the type of person that is easily swayed by the opinions of others, or the "experts" on TV, then this system is not for you. If you like the way establishment tends to handle things, then you will probably not like me. What I do and what the "experts" on TV and the financial advisors will tell you to do are usually very different. I have tried to help several friends make money that got in an investment too late and got out too late because they were too scared not to listen to the experts on TV. As a result, the people I have tried to help invest in the past have often lost money on the same investments that I made money with.

If you are still with me, and you are one of these independent people that can and do swim against the tide of the masses if you think that you are right and that they are wrong, then there is a different problem we need to talk about with you. It is best for you to "paper trade" for a while until you are sure you have the hang of this system. Paper trading is when you pretend to trade and keep up with your results, but you aren't using real money yet. Often independent people get a little too independent and jump right in head-first. Even though you may catch on quickly, there is something about experience that can't be rushed. So in the beginning, go slow- paper trade, and when you do start using real money, only invest in small amounts initially. You don't want to jump in head-first with all the money you have and then find out you didn't quite understand a thing or two.

This is especially true with investments in the Aggressive Investing Funds. Some of the investments I recommend here are considered very aggressive by some people's standards, so please paper trade them first. One of the biggest criticisms of my method by those who use standard investing methods is that I recommend some very aggressive methods.

This may be true. Some of the investments in the aggressive funds do tend to be pretty aggressive. Please paper trade first, start slow, and invest in less aggressive funds until you get a feel for the system.

THE EXPERTS AREN'T EXPERTS EITHER

One of the reasons I ended up doing my own investing is that I found out that the people we rely on to handle our money aren't actually experts at handling our money. I am not trying to put down any brokers or financial advisors, for we all have to make a living, but what I discovered is that these guys are really just salesmen.

What happens is that brokers and financial advisors are trained basically in the rules of their trade and the laws and guidelines of investing, and then they are trained on how to get clients. These guys are very rarely trained in or know much about investing at all. Their job is to get you as a client, then the higher ups in the company tell them which investments to sell you.

Your broker or advisor gets a percent of the money you invest with them. They don't want you to ever take that money out, no matter what is going on in the market, because if you do, they lose money, and so does their company. The idea that you should always stay in the market "no matter what" came from these large companies. It is not for your benefit that they say this. It is for the benefit of the company and for the benefit of your advisor. Big companies have pushed this idea for so long that it has become a common thought in the world of investing, and is taken as "the gospel truth" by many people.

Remember that even those we are taught to see as "experts" at growing your money usually are not. What they *are* good at is getting clients, selling investments to those clients and keeping those clients from ever leaving those investments.

The criticisms I have gotten so far are mostly from financial investors that do not like what I say. I do not blame them. Not all of them are bad. They have to make a living too. Notice though they tend to not argue with me about results. Instead, they tend to argue about my way of doing things, things that in theory goes against what they were taught and is therefore considered bad. The problem is that they are all arguing theories and academic

14

definitions. I am not about to argue with them about those things. My argument is based on one thing and one thing only- results. I don't care how many big words you can use, how many years you spent in school, or how many clients you have- my only question is how good are your results?

THIS IS NOT DAY TRADING

Some of you may be looking for a "get-rich-quick" type of system. This system is not for you. This is not day trading, and it is nothing excessively risky. This is a SYSTEM of handling and growing your money as quickly as you can safely do it. The ultimate goal is to live off your money instead of *having* to work for your money. I am going to show you how to put the money you are working for to work for you. I am going to show you how to turn the money you are earning into more and more money until you can eventually get out of the "rat race" and live off of your investments. When you get to this point, you can still work if you *want* to, but you don't *have* to. If you do still decide to work, you can do what you *want* to do, not what you *have* to do.

Most people make money and then they spend it all. This is the normal average. They work hard for their money, but then only get to spend that money *once*. You are going to learn how to "earn" the money once, but spend it *forever*. You are going to start taking some of the money you physically earn, invest it, turn it into more money, and eventually make enough off of your "money generator" that you can live off your money instead of having to earn every dime forever. You are going to start putting some of that money into investments to make that money *work for you* instead of *you working for it*. Eventually, when you have enough money invested, you will be able to live off the interest you earn off of that investment.

Say you save up a million dollars, and say you make 10% per year on your money, which is about average, your money is now earning you $100,000 per year without you doing much of anything. You never touch the base one million dollars; you only spend the interest that spins off of it. You now have a money tree. You pick its leaves, but leave the rest of the tree alone.

The SYSTEM I am going to show you is kind of a "medium term" investment system. It is not day trading, you are not going to be getting in and out of your investments all the time. But it is also not exactly a long-term system either. Your focus *is* on long-term

16

growth of your money, but if a position you are in starts plummeting, we are not going to stay on a sinking ship. We are going to find the quickest rising investments and ride them like an elevator upwards, then get off when the elevator slows or reverses and jump on the next elevator that is rising quicker than the others.

IF THIS STUFF WORKS, WHY DO I NEED TO WRITE BOOKS?

This is a very, very good question, and you should always ask this question of anyone claiming to have any kind of secret money making knowledge. Here is my answer:

I'm not where I want to be yet. It's as simple as that. I do feel like I have a good, solid, safe system. I do feel like it is *much* safer than letting someone else handle my money. I do feel like I make great returns, and have grown a small amount of money into a much larger pile. BUT, it takes money to make more money. I started trying to figure this system out maybe ten or fifteen years ago. I got bruised and roughed up as I went. I lost a lot of money along the way. I learned as I went. I kept studying. I kept trying, and now I feel pretty confident that my system is at least as good as any body else's out there that I have come across, but much easier and simpler to actually do. You won't need a PhD or a business degree to follow, though you will need some will power, determination and some general "stick-with-it-ness" in order to get by the early stages of growing your money.

The beginning is the hardest. You don't have much, and the less you have the slower the growth you will see, and that's just not exciting. But once it starts to grow, it gets fun. There are still times along the way when you will get frustrated, irritated, angry, scared and you will wish the market would just climb up gradually and consistently and stop stalling, falling, jumping around, and all the other things it tends to do. If you stick with it, when the smoke clears, the long-term picture is great. If you get impatient and impulsive you can really mess up the long-term picture.

So again, why listen to me? If I were that good with stocks I wouldn't have to publish a book! The answer is that I just am not retired yet. I am still plagued by the tyranny of money, but I am climbing out of that pit. I got a late start in investing, it took me years to start doing well, and now I am making up for lost time. But money makes money. I need more money from writing so that

I have more money to invest so I can get to my own goal of retiring early, living off my investments, and doing the work I *want* to do.

I also very much enjoy learning and helping others with what I have learned.

NOBODY CARES FOR YOUR MONEY AS MUCH AS YOU DO

Ken Roberts, a famous self-investment guru used to say this a lot. And it is completely true. Nobody cares about your money as much as you do. NOBODY! I figured this out the hard way. And I have watched several friends also figure this out the hard way. Look at all the financial scandals that were in the news the last few years- AIG, Bernie Madoff, and the housing crisis to give just a few examples. Your best interests are not anywhere on the priority lists of these guys at all, much less at the top of their priorities. But examples of why you need to manage your own money don't even have to be on such a grandiose scale.

I have three friends that would have retired very comfortably had it not been for the stock market plummet right after the terrorist attacks of 9/11, and if their financial advisor would have taken them out of the market as directed. One lady, as an example, who had recently lost her husband, had about a million dollars saved and invested. When the market started going down she asked her financial advisor to take her out of the market for a while, maybe put her in something safe like a money market or bonds or something. The advisor spoke down to her and basically refused to take her money out as she requested. When the smoke cleared her nest egg of a million dollars had dropped to somewhere around $250,000. Now, instead of enjoying her retirement as she had earned the right to do, she is really having to watch her money, and even ended up having to take a part time job to get by. She is in her 70s and still has to work.

I have other very similar stories that I won't bore you with, but the point of the story is that NOBODY CARES ABOUT YOUR MONEY AS MUCH AS YOU DO!! The bottom line for me is that if you want someone who *truly* cares about your financial future to control your money, then that person needs to be you. There are two advantages to being in control of your money. First, you do not have to pay anybody else fees to manage your money; therefore you get to keep more of it. Secondly, YOU control when and if you need to take your money out and sit on the sidelines a bit in order to protect your nest egg. This is a huge point. Sometimes it is knowing when to be *out* of the market that determines how much money you retire with.

I believe you can make the same (if not better) returns on your money as the "experts" offer with this simple system, and much more safely, because *you* are in charge. Even if you didn't make quite the same returns as the experts, just knowing when to get out of the market, and having control of your money so that you could make that happen if necessary would still be a tremendous advantage.

INDIAN RETIREMENT INVESTING

I met a young lady from India at a seminar a few years back and we started talking about investing. As I was telling her about the system I use, and about my theory of spending money forever instead of spending it only once she got really excited. Evidently, this idea is a given among the people of India. They work hard and save as much money as they can when they are young. When they get enough money saved, they buy a business (like a dry cleaning business) and hire people to run it for them, often younger family members. Then they retire and live off the income from the business, which they don't even have to physically work in. They have turned money that they earned into a money generator. This is how they save for retirement.

I look at investing the same way- as a business. You work hard, save your money and then you invest that money. When you invest, you are actually buying shares of companies. As these companies make profits, you share in the profits. Profits you don't have to work for. The companies you have shares in are doing the work. This is passive income. Income you are not physically working for. You are taking your hard earned money and putting it into a money generator, just like Indian retirees do.

I like my way better though. What I like better about my business is that I don't have to hire any employees as the Indians do when they buy a physical business. The more employees you have the more headaches you have. Ask any business owner. You may love your employees to death, but they still complicate things. You have to find them, you have to train them, and you have to find replacements when they are sick or when they quit.

But the overall idea is the same, whether you retire like the Indians by buying a physical business, or like I do, by buying shares of companies. Either way, you work hard, save your money and buy a money generator with your hard earned cash instead of spending it all.

HOW MUCH DO YOU NEED TO RETIRE ON?

In order to know how much money you need to start saving to retire comfortably, it helps to know how much you want to live on when you retire. Most people estimate that they want to retire on a million dollars. If you have a million dollars in investments, and your investments average 8-10% returns over the long run, as the overall stock market usually does, then you will be living on around eighty to a hundred thousand dollars per year. All without ever touching the million you saved up. Year after year, that million you put into your money generator should yield you an average of around a hundred thousand dollars. All without you physically working.

To figure out just how much you need to put in now to reach that goal, we are going to go online to a retirement calculator. We are going to use that online calculator to estimate just how much money we need to invest every month to reach your retirement goal. On this calculator, you will input your current age, the age you want to retire at, and how much you want to retire on. The calculator will then tell you how much you need to invest every month to reach that goal.

Here is the website of my favorite retirement calculator: http://www.bloomberg.com/personal-finance/calculators/retirement/

And here is a screenshot with an example calculation:

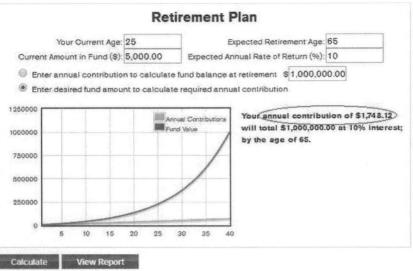

In the above example, I used 25 as your current age, $5000 as the starting amount, 65 as the retirement age, and one million as the goal. Of course, you need to put your own information in. Your own age (I'm not 25, not by a long shot), starting amount, goal amount, etc. But I would like you to use 65 as your retirement age and 10% as your estimated returns. With those numbers above, you would have to invest $1,748.12 per year to retire a millionaire at age 65. That comes to $146 per month, about $37 per week. Nice, right? The older you are when you start, the quicker that number goes up! So start young!

Based on your own numbers, write the yearly, monthly and weekly amount you need to put away for retirement here:

Yearly Amount	
Monthly Amount	
Bi-Weekly Amount	
Weekly Amount	

Why do I want you to list 65 as your retirement age, and one million dollars (or whatever makes you happy) as your retirement goal? We are hoping to retire earlier than 65, and with more money than that if possible. But for now, we are calculating a BARE BONES number that tells us what we *have* to put away on a regular basis for us to reach the minimum goal of retirement at the minimum age of 65 with a minimum of one million dollars (or whatever amount you chose). Many of you will also have social security to rely on, some of you will have pensions. Here, we are simply trying to find a bare bones minimum we need to retire on as if social security and pensions don't exist. We are actually going to do something later to try and accelerate the process, but if all else fails, we want a bare minimum amount by a bare minimum time period.

The number your calculations come up with is now a new bill for you. It is a bill you pay every single month, as if it were a utility bill or a car payment. Come Hell or high water, you pay that amount to your retirement fund. It is non negotiable. Later we are going to have another investment fund we use to try to speed things up a bit more- A LOT MORE. But your Retirement Fund is your bare minimum investment fund for retiring comfortably, and it is a bill. You can pay weekly, every other week or monthly. Whatever is easiest for you. But pay every time.

There are three things you can do to really speed up how soon you can save up a nest egg big enough for retirement. The first thing you can do is start investing when you are young. The second is to start investing when you are young. And the third is to start investing when you are young. It is really that important! Make it a priority while you are young. Unfortunately, most people don't get any financial common sense until much later in life. I include myself here.

If you are reading this book and you are no longer young, all is not lost. I just really want to emphasize to the younger crowd how easy all this becomes if they start early.

If you want more help on using the retirement calculator, go to the members area on the investing area of www.MatthewBarnes-101.com and watch video tutorial number one. Again, the password is QUAN

SETTING UP YOUR RETIREMENT FUND

Let's take that money you are now ready to be putting away CONSISTENTLY, like a bill for your retirement, and put it somewhere it can grow. Remember that what I'm about to tell you is my opinion. It is what I do myself. But neither I nor anybody else can promise you that you will never lose money or that what has worked in the past will work in the future. That being said, this is what I do with my own money, which tells you how much I believe in what I'm about to say.

First though, there are three preliminary things we need to get done. First, please go to Yahoo.com and create a free portfolio to track your investments. You can find this under Yahoo Finance. It seems to be the best free portfolio tracker, in my opinion. Here is a link- I circled and pointed an arrow at the Finance link at the side of the page:

Next, go to "My Portfolio". I have circled and pointed an arrow at the correct ink:

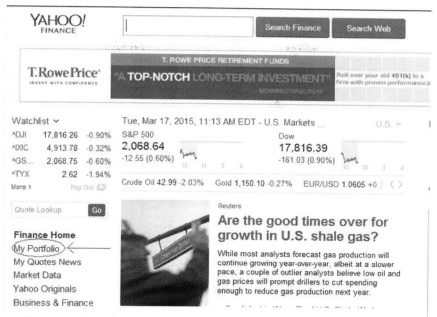

Once there, you can name your portfolio, add stocks and ETFs to the portfolio and basically keep track how your investments are doing. Or even keep track of how the investments you are watching but are not in yet are doing.

Below is a screen shot of an example Yahoo portfolio with a few investments entered. This is not my portfolio; this is one of the portfolios I use to keep up with investments I am interested in, and how they are doing over the long term. If an investment I am not in is consistently and soundly tromping an investment I am in, I switch investments.

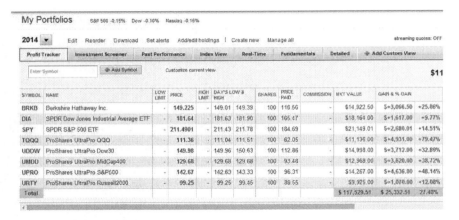

Reprinted with permission © Yahoo.com. All rights reserved.

To enter investments you want to track, or investments you are in, enter the symbol into the symbol area and push the "Add Symbol" button. To enter how much of an investment you own, hit the edit button you see beside 2014 in the top left corner. This will take you to a screen with a button at the bottom titled Add / Edit holdings data. After you push that button you can enter the amount of stocks you bought and at what price you paid.

It is best if you "paper trade" first. Simply pretend you are investing, but without money. Add the stock symbol I am going to tell you about to your portfolio and pretend you are in it. Whether you are in it for real, or paper trading first, please be patient. The stock market doesn't go straight up. Even in a stock that makes 100% in one year, there are times it is dipping or stalling sideways. This is one of the reasons to paper trade. When it is real money you get scared and impatient easier, especially if this is new to you.

The second preliminary is to open a Scottrade account. If you have another online brokerage account you prefer that is fine. I simply use Scottrade and know how to tell you to use it so that is what I'm suggesting. If you have trouble opening a Scottrade account, simply call them up and let them walk you through it. The main menu for opening an account is: https://apply.scottrade.com/?sctr=ms:s2390181:tp_bp:i111041528 63&jsf=0524aadd-3899-4b6f-9e84-2ea9f42736da:33186. Or you

28

can just go to www.Scottrade.com and contact them for assistance if you need it.

When you make payments to your Retirement Fund, Scottrade is where you will be sending your money. Remember, just putting your money into Scottrade doesn't mean it is invested. When you put money in there the money is simply sitting there. It doesn't go into an investment until you place an order to buy a specific investment. We will go over that shortly.

Some people are afraid of doing their own investing; they have heard horror stories of other people playing with stocks and losing a lot of money, or something similar. What we are doing is going to be different, so don't fear. And don't freak out when you send your first check to Scottrade. The money is not invested until you place an order. Also, Scottrade is free to have your money in. The only charges are when you place orders. There may be a minimum required balance though.

The last preliminary is to go to http://bigcharts.marketwatch.com/ or www.StockCharts.com and get familiar with playing with stock charts. For now, just get familiar with looking at stock charts on these sites. A little later I'm going to teach you how to read the charts in a very simple way. All the charts I am using will be from www.StockCharts.com. I used to use Yahoo's free chart service, but they changed it too often and too much for me. I also used Big Charts quite a bit, but they would not give me permission to use their charts in this book. For this reason, I now prefer www.StockCharts.com, which is a great site, with friendly people.

If you want more help on this subject, go to the members area on the investing area of www.MatthewBarnes-101.com and watch video tutorial numbers three, four and five. Again, the password is QUAN

WHAT TO INVEST IN FOR RETIREMENT

Like I alluded to earlier, we are actually going to have two investment funds. The first investment fund is going to be our Retirement Fund. We have calculated how much money we need to input per month into an investment averaging around 8-10% per year so that we can retire at the age of 65 with a million dollars (or whatever age you chose and whatever amount you estimated you needed to retire comfortably). We are going to pay this amount per month into our Retirement Fund as if it were a bill. This is the money we are relying on to make sure we can retire in comfort, and we are going to invest it safely and conservatively.

The second investment fund, which we will go over soon, is going to be somewhat aggressive. It is going to be the fund we use to try and retire earlier than the age of sixty-five, and with more than a million dollars (or whatever you estimated you wanted to retire on). We won't be investing as safely with this Early Retirement Fund- though I have never really lost money in this fund either. What I put in this fund simply moves very fast, so you have more potential to make more money faster. We put money into the Retirement Fund like a bill, but we only use excess money, after all the bills are paid, for the second, more aggressive Early Retirement Fund.

I would like to take a second to re-emphasize what I just said. Critics of my system often take issue with my Aggressive Fund as if it is the only Fund I suggest. But the Aggressive Fund uses excess money, after all the bills are paid. It is the Fund we use to try to improve upon our main retirement fund. The Aggressive Fund is not the main fund. Most of your money will go into the Retirement Fund. The idea is to do your best to guarantee a nice retirement. With that being established we then use an Aggressive Fund to try and speed things up as much as possible.

For the Retirement Fund, my favorite investment is Berkshire Hathaway (stock symbol BRKB). Berkshire Hathaway is the company of investing all-star Warren Buffett. Buffett is the Michael Jordan of investing. Nobody can do what he does. It is currently 2015, and over the past four years or so I estimate his company has made right at a 30% return per year. That is phenomenal! Nobody does that. The S&P 500 usually makes around 10% per year, and most investors will tell you that you really can't do better than that. Buffett does. Regularly. So if you can't beat him, join him. Buffett reportedly invests every dollar of his money into his company. You know if he does that, he is serious about making the company profitable.

My advice is to take your Retirement Fund money, pay it as a bill to your Scottrade account, and every time you build up $500 or more, buy as much BRKB as you can. Don't worry about trying to time your entry, just buy more every chance you get. The reason you want to save up to $500 or more each time you buy shares of his company is that it will cost you $7 each time you buy. This is how Scottrade makes its money. The fee is not $7 per share you buy; it is $7 per transaction. If you buy shares every time you get $50, after ten transactions you have put in $500, but paid $70 in fees. If instead you save up and buy $500 of BRKB at once, your fees only total $7.

If Warren Buffett dies or seems to be losing his abilities I may change my mind in the future, but for now, while he's alive and healthy, it is my opinion that you stock up on his investments. He is truly a superstar. Notice that for your Retirement Fund we estimated you making 10% per year to retire at 65. If Buffett keeps going as he has in the past, you may retire earlier than you thought. We estimated the 8-10% to retire at 65 as a bare bones minimum.

Neither I nor anyone else can guarantee Buffett or any of the other good investors out there will keep doing what they have done in the past, so keep that in mind. As long as Buffett is doing as well as he is now, I plan on using him for my Retirement Fund.

AN ALTERNATE RETIREMENT FUND INVESTMENT IDEA

I personally have my retirement money invested in BRKB. I do it exactly as I am telling you to do. Many people will tell you to invest in a wide variety of companies, but this isn't how the really rich seem to do it, and its not what has served me best. Spreading your money out too widely dilutes your gains. Warren Buffett has all his money in his own company, Berkshire Hathaway, and many other very rich people do the same. They concentrate their money into All-Star Funds. If the smartest investor in the world is doing it, so am I.

One caveat- if you are going to invest mostly in a single stock, which I don't really recommend, make sure it is a safe stock. I would not invest in any stock not listed in the Dow, the S&P or the Nasdaq. I would also make sure the stock is not going through any mergers as well. In short, I really wouldn't invest my Retirement Fund Money too much in single stocks- too much can happen to a single stock.

ETFs, which I will talk about more in a minute, are much more diverse and safe. Even though you are buying one investment when you buy an ETF, it covers a wide variety of companies, so you don't have to worry about mergers and things like that as you would with an individual stock.

The same thing goes for investing in Berkshire Hathaway (BRKB). Even though Berkshire Hathaway is a single company, it is a company that invests in other companies. So even though you are buying one investment, you are really investing in the 10 or 12 investments Berkshire Hathaway are invested in.

There are two ways to make money off your investments. The first way is if you buy the stock at a low price (say $5 per share) and then sell the stock at a higher price (say $20 per share). The other way to make money is by Dividends. Dividends are like getting a percent of the company's profits. You are part owner of the company, and when they make a profit you get a tiny bit of it.

If you don't like the idea of all your retirement money going into one place, high dividend investing is another idea. There is a website called Dividend Detective (http://www.dividenddetective.com/) where stocks and ETFs (exchange traded funds) are ranked according to who has the highest dividends. Right now, a dividend of three, four or five percent per year is actually considered pretty good. Yet there are ETFs out there making MUCH more than that. None of them make quite as good returns as Berkshire Hathaway's average of 30% lately, but some of them break 10% at least.

Even with dividend investing, I prefer ETFs to individual stocks. ETFs are Exchange Traded Funds. They are like Mutual Funds in that they are a mixture of a lot of different companies instead of just one. When you buy shares of one ETF, you are actually investing in dozens of entities- this is how I only have a few investments, but actually diversify at the same time. Mutual Funds have lots of fees, and if the fund goes down you can't get right back out without paying more fees. ETFs are just like Mutual Funds, but without the fees, and you can trade them freely like a stock. So if you are wrong about an ETF you get in, you can get back out easily and not have to pay penalties like you might if you were investing in Mutual Funds.

One of my favorite dividend investments in the past is a REIT with the stock symbol REM. A REIT is a Real Estate Investment Trust. There is a story behind these. Evidently the rich used to invest in Real Estate Trust Funds years ago, which paid out very high dividends. At some point the government changed a law that made it easier for those of us that aren't filthy rich to invest in these Trusts. As long as these Trusts pay out most of their taxable gains as dividends to their shareholders, they are allowed to pay very low taxes. For this reason, REM, and other REITS like REM, offer much higher dividends than other investments. REM usually pays somewhere between 10-15% per year, and is usually at the top of my list of safe high dividend investments.

Dividends usually pay out every three months. Say you have a million dollars invested in REM, and say REM is paying out 10% per year. That means you are making a hundred thousand dollars per year on dividends. You would receive about twenty five thousand dollars every three months- usually in March, June, September and December. Remember too, you are spending that million dollars forever. The dividends are created from the million you have invested. You don't actually spend any of that million. Ever. That million is your money tree. You don't want to chop down that tree.

If you want to invest your Retirement Fund in something other than Berkshire Hathaway, or want to split your money between at least two different investments, think about investing in an investment with a high dividend return like REM. In order to do your own research, go http://www.dividenddetective.com/dividend_etfs.htm to search for a dividend producing ETF that may be doing even better than REM.

Here is a screen shot of the top ten dividend producing ETFs as of February 19, 2015.

HIGH-DIVIDEND ETFs

You've heard about the advantages of using exchange-traded-funds (ETFs) to hop on and off market sector swings. But you might be surprised to learn than many ETFs pay high dividend yields (dividend yield is the next 12-month's estimated dividends divided by the price you pay for the shares).

For instance, more than 50 ETFs are paying at least 3% yields and more than 20 are paying 5% or higher.

Here's a list of all known dividend-paying ETFs, sorted by yield with the highest dividend ETFs at the top. We're still refining our techniques for validating dividend yield data, so verify everything.

Too many ETFs, too little time? Click here to subscribe to Dividend Detective

Top Yielding ETFs — Page 1 of 9

Rank	ETF Name	ETF Symbol	ETF Category	Recent Yield*
#1	iShares MSCI UAE Capped ETF	UAE		27.50%
#2	iShares Mortgage Real Estate Capped ETF	REM	Real Estate	12.55%
#3	SPDR S&P International Telecommunications Sector ETF	IST	Technology	12.54%
#4	ProShares Global Listed Private Equity ETF	PEX	Miscellaneous	12.47%
#5	Mortgage REIT Income ETF	MORT	Income	10.09%
#6	BDC Income ETF	BIZD	Income	8.27%
#7	PowerShares KBW High Dividend Yield Financial Portfolio	KBWD	Income	8.06%
#8	PowerShares CEF Income Composite Portfolio	PCEF	Value	7.31%
#9	Junior MLP ETF	MLPJ	Energy	6.86%
#10	Multi-Asset Diversified Income Index Fund	MDIV	Income	6.79%

Reprinted with permission © DivdendDetective.com. All rights reserved.

Notice that currently REM is at number two, with 12.55% per year. UAE is number one at a whopping 27.5%. Always look into these

34

companies and confirm these dividend numbers for yourself before you buy a large amount of them. Also, I am familiar with REM, so I am comfortable investing in it, but I am not familiar with UAE. If I were going to invest in that ETF, I'd look up information about the company first. 27.5% is very large. Sometimes companies offer higher dividends if the company is less stable to get people to invest. REM is high because it is a REIT, we need to know why UAE is so high before we sink our hard earned cash into it, or rely on it for retirement.

ONE OTHER THING ABOUT DIVIDENDS- if you plan on buying shares of a company like REM, make sure that their chart looks good (we will go over that soon). If you are making 10% dividends on REM, but the price of REM drops 15% per year, you are still losing money.

As of this writing, investing in REM is a little shaky. I have invested in REM in the past, and would do so again, but right now the price of REM is dropping too much.

Some people buy a dividend producing investment and never plan on getting out. Ever. If you plan on doing this, REM is still ok. Otherwise, I would search Dividend Detective for the highest dividend yielding investment that also has a chart that is going up, or at least moving sideways.

If you get into an investment that pays good dividends, AND is going up, then you make money in two different ways. This is ideal.

Again, we will go over very basic chart reading in a minute.

If you want more help on this subject, go to the members area on the investing area of www.MatthewBarnes-101.com and watch video tutorial number six. Again, the password is QUAN

YOUR FUN FUND AND EARLY RETIREMENT FUND

You might not like this part so much at first, but you will once you get used to it.

For one month, ONLY buy your necessities. Only buy those things you absolutely positively HAVE to have to survive. Water bill, electric bill, health insurance, things like that. It is OK to include a basic cable bill if you want, and maybe Internet and cell phones- you can decide on whether or not to include these things as necessities. But new shoes, manicures, new clothing, new hunting equipment, new tools, eating out or any other thing you buy for PLEASURE is *not* counted as a bill. Try, for one month, to not spend any money on anything but these necessities. At the end of the month when you get your bank statement, it will tell you how much money you made and how much you spent (hopefully just on necessities).

Whatever money you have left over after paying for your necessities is now "EXCESS" money- money in excess of what you absolutely positively have to have in order to survive. You want as much "Excess" money as you can get, because that's the money you get to have fun with. We are going to take your excess money and divide it between another Retirement Fund and "Fun Money". Fun Money is the money you can spend on things you like but don't necessarily need.

Please note that our ultimate goal is to have the two retirement funds- the safe retirement fund and the much more aggressive retirement fund. First though, we will be taking the excess money that will ultimately be going to the aggressive retirement fund and using it to pay off credit cards and other smaller debts you may have, and then using that money to build up a cash savings for emergencies. Once both of those are done, then that excess money will be rolled into a more Aggressive Investing Fund. Again, we are going to start off conservatively- prepare for retirement and reduce debt- and then once we are in a safe position, then we will start to invest aggressively. This aggressive investing does not replace our general Retirement Fund- it is in addition to our safe Retirement Fund.

Most people actually spend money on what they want first and hope that they can still pay their bills at the end of the month. This is one reason why so many people get behind, live paycheck-to-paycheck, stress over money all the time and stay in debt. We are going to do the opposite. We are going to pay our necessities first, and use the money left over after paying bills to have fun with, reduce debt and ultimately speed up our retirement. If you seem to have no money left over after paying for necessities, then you may need to look at what you see as "necessities". The only ways to increase excess money is to decrease your living costs, make more money, or both.

The Retirement Fund money we calculated as a bill is our safe, secure, retirement fund. We put that money into something safe so that we are fairly well assured that if nothing else, we should be able to retire at 65 comfortably. But we are also going to take some of our "excess" money and ultimately use it to invest a bit more aggressively. The goal is to have one investment fund geared towards playing it safe, but another fund, driven by excess money, that will be invested more aggressively with the hopes of speeding up our retirement, and saving up more than a million (or whatever amount you chose). We will call this investment fund the Early Retirement Fund. Remember, the Retirement Fund is our main investment, where we are trying to secure a good, comfortable retirement at a decent age. The Early Retirement Fund will be in addition to the regular Retirement Fund, and the goal here is to try and hit a few home runs.

So you are going to pay only necessities for a month. When the bank statement comes in, you are going to subtract the money you spent on necessities from the money you made. The remaining amount is your excess money. Now we are going to split that excess money between having fun, and speeding up our retirement. If I were you, I'd invest 30% of it into the Early Retirement Fund and keep the remaining 70% for Fun. You shouldn't be so spartan in hoping for a good future that you don't enjoy the life you have now. So spend some money, have fun, but ALSO invest for the future.

You can play with the percents until you get it where you like it. If you are married, as I am, I suggest doing what my wife and I do- we split the 70% fun money three ways- I get a third, she gets a third and we put a third into a "Big Fun Fund" for vacations, buying a large screen TV and more expensive fun things like that that are really for both of us. By doing this, you each have your own fun money to spend on things you like.

If she wants a new dress, she can get it, as long as she has enough fun money. If he wants a new knife, he can get it, as long as he has enough fun money. No bickering over what the other buys. Each person's fun money is theirs to do as they wish. But you can't spend more on fun than you have in your account. No credit, no getting in debt, even with yourself. From now on, however much fun money you have is simply how much fun money you can spend. If you don't have enough fun money, you need to save up, make more money or cut your necessities.

This way of managing your money also becomes a game. When you see that the less you spend on your bills the more money you have for buying fun things, the more you want to live frugally. You will want to cut costs so that you will have more fun money to do and buy things with.

THE CALCULATION (simple method)- Here is an example calculation:
Pretend this is February and you just got January's bank statement.

Income for January	**$1,000**
minus Necessities for January	**$600**
(add back Fun Money and Early Retirement Money Spent In January)*	**$0**
equals Excess Money for January	**$400**

EXCESS MONEY FOR JANUARY	$400
Early Retirement Fund Money (30%)	$120
Fun Money (70%)	$280

TOTAL FUN MONEY	$280
Spouse A Fun Money (33%)	$84
Spouse B Fun Money (33%)	$84
Big Fun Money (33%)	$84

* Let's say we are calculating January's Fun and Early Retirement money. You don't get the bank statement until February. So any Fun Money or Early Retirement Fund money from January will be spent in February. When you get to March, if you don't account for the Fun and Early Retirement money you spent in February, then those payments will look like necessities/bills in February's calculations, even though they are not. The first Month you do this system, there will be no Fun or Early Retirement money from the previous month, so that number would just be zero. From then on though you will need to keep up with how much Fun and Early Retirement money you paid out that month so you can account for it in your calculations.

*If you want more help on this subject, go to the members area on the investing area of www.MatthewBarnes-101.com and watch video tutorial number two. Again, the password is QUAN. The next two chapters cover other ways of doing these calculations. They are covered under the same video- video tutorial number two,.

A LITTLE MORE COMPLICATED, BUT THOROUGH

In this chapter, I want to go over another way of doing the same calculations for finding your Excess Money, Fun Money and Early Retirement Money, but by using Quicken or some other computerized check register. This is the method my wife and I use, and the one I recommend to really stay on top of things.

This method does take more work than the last, but it is still simple. Once or twice a month, whatever you prefer, you simply keep up with your Expenses verses Income. Then you calculate your Fun and Early Retirement money.

Here is an example calculation:

Starting Balance in Quicken	$1,000
Ending Balance after you pay all the bills due and make all the deposits you have to make	$1,400
Excess Money (Ending Balance – Starting Balance)	$400

The rest of the calculations are the same as before:

EXCESS MONEY	**$400**
Early Retirement Fund Money (30%)	$120`
Fun Money (70%)	$280

TOTAL FUN MONEY	**$280**
Spouse A Fun Money (33%)	$84
Spouse B Fun Money (33%)	$84
Big Fun Money (33%)	$84

Here is the magic of using Quicken. You can make "slush funds" for "Early Retirement Fund", "His Fun Money", "Her Fun Money" and "Big Fun Money". To do this, enter a transaction for each of those Fun Money Categories, but make the date a few years from now. Quicken will draw a line showing transactions up until today's date, and put those "slush funds" after today's date.

Here is an example Quicken Register:

Date	Num	Payee / Category	Memo	Payment Exp	Clr	Deposit	Balance
2/8/15		Netflix / TV		8 75			4,119 08
2/9/15		Deposit / Salary				322 25	4,441 33
2/9/15	v	Raceway / Car	gas	43 00			4,398 33
2/9/15	v	Jack's / Groceries		22 17			4,376 16
2/13/15		Deposit / Salary				628 77	5,004 93
2/13/15	v	Kroger / Car	gas	24 00			4,980 93
2/14/15		Farm Bureau Car Insurance / Car Insurance		127 00			4,853 93
2/16/15	v	Sunrise Market / Car	gas	46 68			4,807 25
2/16/15	v	Sunrise Market / Groceries		2 28			4,804 97
2/17/15		Hulu / TV		7 99			4,796 98
2/18/15	v	Walmart / Groceries		31 10			4,765 88
2/18/15	v	Kroger / Car	gas	15 00			4,750 88
1/28/21		CC, Debt, Savings, Early Retirement Fund / Slush Fund					4,750 88
1/29/21		A's Fun Fund / Fun Fund		35 00			4,715 88
1/30/21		B's Fun Fund / Fun Fund		50 00			4,665 88
1/31/21		Big Fun Fund / Fun Fund					4,665 88
8/20/15	Num	Payee / Category	Memo	Payment Exp		Deposit	

Current Balance:	4,750.88	Ending Balance:	4,665.88

Notice that the bold line denotes today's date. When keeping up with balances go by the "Ending Balance" which tells your balance up until today's date. The "Current Balance" is higher because it doesn't take off the Slush Funds we put in at future dates.

Notice the slush funds under the bold line for "CC, Debt, Savings and Early Retirement", "Spouse A's Fun Fund", "Spouse B's Fun Fund" and a "Big Fun Fund". Whenever you get more "Early Retirement Money" or "Fun Money" you just add that amount to the slush funds you already have. Whenever you send a check in to invest from your "Early Retirement Fund", or spend "Fun Money", you simply deduct that amount from the correct slush fund. Easy.

Don't forget to keep up with ALL your receipts, deposit slips and checks written so you have all the information. If you buy something with fun money, make sure to write on the receipt which Fun Fund it comes out of. Also, balance your checkbook once a month when you get your bank statement (Quicken calls this Reconciling). This way of doing bills allows you to stay on top of your money better. You know where every little bit goes.

If you want more help on this subject, go to the members area on www.MatthewBarnes-101.com and watch video tutorial number two. Again, the password is QUAN

ONE MORE WAY

Doing finances can be complicated. I want to offer you one more way of doing the same thing we just did in the last two chapters- figuring out how much money we have in excess of our necessities, and then allocating the excess money to both an Accelerated Early Retirement Fund and also to a Fun Fund.

Like in the last method, we are going to use Quicken. Enter your bills and deposits during the month. Any money you spend as Fun Money or Early Retirement Money is labeled that way in the Quicken transaction and taken out of Slush Funds just like in the last chapter.

Instead of keeping up with the starting balance before you do bills and the ending balance when you are done, this time just enter your bills as you go and at the end of the month simply go to the "Reports" tab on Quicken, hit "Easy Answer Reports and Graphs" and hit "where did I spend my money last month".

A report will pop up telling you how much money went into your account, how much came out and will even subtract the money that went in versus the money that came out for you and give you your Excess Money for the month.

Here is an example report:

Cash Flow Report
2/1/15 Through 2/28/15

Category Description	2/1/15- 2/28/15
INFLOWS	
Salary	1,888.98
TOTAL INFLOWS	1,888.98
OUTFLOWS	
Car	193.18
Car Insurance	127.00
Car Tags	24.74
Early Retirement Fund	100.00
Entertainment	16.41
Fun Money	60.00
Groceries	131.32
Health Insurance	303.00
Insurance	25.00
Rent	500.00
TV	16.74
Utilities	81.53
TOTAL OUTFLOWS	1,578.92
OVERALL TOTAL	310.06

This report says that in February you brought in $1888.98 and spent $1578.92, leaving you with $310.06 in Excess Money. Before you split that money between Early Retirement Money and Fun Money, we need to do one more thing.

Notice that under OUTFLOWS in the picture above, $100 was sent to your Early Retirement Fund and $60 was spent from your Fun Fund during the month. These should have been subtracted from your Early Retirement Slush Fund and your Fun Fund as you entered bills during the month.

The $160 from the Early Retirement Fund Money and Fun Money combined needs to be added back to your Overall Excess Money. If you don't do this, the Retirement Fund Money and Fun Money that you spent that month will be counted as a bill even though they are not, and have already been accounted for in the slush funds.

The $160 is now added to the $310.06 total excess money is giving you your actual Excess Money for that month, which is $470.06. You then split that amount between Early Retirement and Fun.

30% of $470.06 is $141, and that is added to your Early Retirement Slush Fund in Quicken. The rest, $329 is split three ways and added to the three Fun Funds. This basically comes to $110 each.

In Table Form:

Excess Money for the Month	$310.06
+ Early Retirement Money Spent	$100
+ Fun Money Spent	$60
ACTUAL EXCESS MONEY	$470.06

EXCESS MONEY	$470.06
Early Retirement Money (30%)	$141
Fun Money (70%)	$329

TOTAL FUN MONEY	$329
Spouse A Fun Money (33%)	$110
Spouse B Fun Money (33%)	$110
Big Fun Fund (33%)	$110

If you want more help on this subject, go to the members area on www.MatthewBarnes-101.com and watch video tutorial number two. Again, the password is QUAN

THE FIRST THING TO DO WITH YOUR EARLY RETIREMENT FUND MONEY

Remember that the meat and potatoes of this system is having two investing funds. The first is a conservative fund we invest safely to try and secure a comfortable retirement. The second is a much more aggressive investing fund we use to try to accelerate the creation of our money tree.

Before we use the Early Retirement Money we just learned to calculate for accelerating retirement, we are first going to use it to pay off debts and save up an emergency cash reserve. I know this is frustrating- you probably want to skip to the aggressive investing, but by doing it the way I am showing, we first build a conservative retirement investment that is working for us, we end up debt free, and we end up with cash reserves for emergencies. Once those things are set up, you are financially on pretty solid ground and you can start risking a bit.

If you start risking before all those things are set up, or try to risk too much with your Retirment Fund, a set-back could be rough. But if you have your financial feet on solid ground, you can tolerate a bit more risk without having to worry about a setback being the end of the world. In other words, secure your survival first, then go for the fence. Don't go for the fence before your survival is secured. Also, never risk your retirement on aggressive investing. You only go after the riskier investing with the excess money we learned to calculate in the last chapter.

You want to obtain a secure future. You want to be on track with your Retirement Fund, have your debt paid down and have an emergency cash reserve. That is a solid position to be in. THEN you can try to "win" by attempting to accelerate your investing.

Secure your future first, then chase your dream. This way, if there are times your aggressive Early Retirment Fund doesn't do as well as you'd like, you are still on very solid ground financially. A setback here and there on your Aggressive Fund will be no big deal. As long as your finances are secure, you can keep aiming for the fence with your Aggressive Fund. If instead you start risking before your financial life is secure, a setback could really cause you trouble.

By saving up a cash emergency fund, in an emergency, we won't need to borrow money from a credit card or other lender that is going to eat you alive with interest. This is what most people do, and they end up getting behind and deeper and deeper in the hole. This is what credit cards want you to do. They want you to get behind and never catch up. This way they loan you money once or twice, and you end up paying them for it for life. You become THEIR money tree. They loan you a small amount, but in the end get paid back WAY more than they ever loaned you. We are trying to work our way to doing the reverse: earning money once, but spending it for life. We want to create our own money tree.

We want to pay off those credit cards and other debts (aside from our mortgage and / or student loans- more on that in a minute) with the Early Retirement Fund money. Once that is done, we want to funnel that money into building up a decent savings account that you can borrow from if you ever have an emergency. This way you are borrowing from yourself in times of emergency. Not only will you borrow from yourself interest free, but you will also be making money on your savings if you park the money into a money market account. You will have become your own bank from which you can borrow when needed. This is much better than borrowing from a credit card and falling into their black hole from which it is hard to escape.

So here is the order so far:
1. We have calculated how much money you need to pay yourself each month to retire comfortably at age 65. This is your Retirement Fund, and you pay it as a bill. I like to invest that money in Berkshire Hathaway (BRKB), or BRKB and REM (or another high paying dividend investment) if we want a little diversification.
2. We have also started keeping up with our bills better. We keep up with our incoming money versus our necessities. What is left over is our excess money. We split the excess

money between Fun Money and an Early Retirement Fund, which we are going to use to try and expedite our retirement.

3. Before we start investing the Early Retirement Fund Money, we need to use the money to pay off our debt and build savings.

4. As we pay our bills, we are going to make the minimum payment to our credit cards. After we pay our bills, we will have excess money, and 30% of that goes into our Early Retirement Account. That Early Retirement Account Money will go as an extra payment to our credit cards or other debt. We do this until the credit card or debt is paid off.

5. The only exceptions to paying off debts first is your house Mortgage and Student Loans. If you wait until those huge loans are paid off you'll be waiting too long before you can begin to invest strongly. So just include those payments as bills and don't worry about trying to pay them off early.

6. Once debt is paid off, funnel the Early Retirement Fund Money into building a savings account. To be safe, build up enough money to live off of for three, six or nine months, depending on how cautious you want to be.

7. Once your savings account is big enough, then it is time to funnel the Early Retirement Fund Money into accelerated investing, which we will go over next. The goal now is to try to speed up your retirement age.

Once again, I want to point out that starting early is HUGE. Unfortunately, most people, like me, don't get enough sense to invest until much later in life. Then it becomes much slower and harder. If you start young you can retire young. And believe me- you want to!!

ACCELERATED INVESTING- HOW TO PICK THE WINNERS
the fastest rising elevator theory

Before I start this chapter, I'd like to address a few points I've been criticized on in earlier versions of this book.

I am a big fan of Warren Buffett. I am a big fan for one reason- he gets great results. Buffett is a fundamental investor. For those of you that are new to the market, a fundamental investor is someone who studies every nook and cranny of a company before they buy stock in that company. They invest in a company only if they think that the company is a very good company. This is one of the two main ways to make decisions.

The other type of investor is a technical investor. A technical investor basically studies chart formations and uses indicators such as up-trends and down-trends to make investing decisions. Technical investors don't tend to study the company much at all. They feel that all they need to know about a company shows up in their stock chart. If a company is strong, prices rise. If a company goes weak, prices fall. I am more of a technical investor. I do look into a company a little bit to make sure they aren't going out of business or anything like that, but for whatever reason, I have always done best using mostly technical indicators. Many people use both fundamentals and technical indicators.

I personally do not care, at all, whether a person is a fundamentalist or a technical trader. I use technical trading because its what I do best with. However, it may not be what other people do best with, and that is fine by me. The only thing I care about is results. The fundamentalists and the technical traders are two opposing philosophies that tend to argue and butt heads constantly over which group is correct. I recommended Warren Buffett's company for the Retirement Fund but I personally use technical trading for my Aggressive, Early Retirement Fund. Several of the more "academic" investors claimed that I was being hypocritical.

They seemed to think I needed to pick one method and only one method.

Years ago, there was an experiment in the markets where a few monkeys were given darts. These darts were thrown at a wall where the name of different stocks were listed. Whichever stocks the monkeys hit with darts were the stocks the researchers bought. In the end, the monkeys' investment portfolio did as good or better than the top ranked analysts of the time.

Here is how much I don't care what method you use- only the results you obtain… if those monkeys continually beat the other guys, I may have used their choices. I only care about results, not the methods used to get them.

Buffett uses fundamentals, and he is an all-star at investing that way. But nobody else gets those results. Nobody. The fundamentalists always point at Buffett as proof that fundamental investing is the way to go, but that is not true. Buffett is simply very good at investing using fundamentals as a tool. Other fundamentalists don't do nearly as good. Other people use other tools and do well. Each person simply has to figure out which tool or tools they are best at using to go after the best returns. For me, I prefer to ride Buffett's investments for my retirement investing, and for my own investing, I have always done best with technical analysis.

That being said, let's move on to the Aggressive, Early Retirement Fund and how to invest in it.

I'm going to assume you have paid off your debt and credit cards and built up a decent savings account that you are happy with. It is now time to start investing your Early Retirement Fund Money and trying to grow it really quick. So how do we pick a winner?

The fastest rising elevator theory-
If you knew which investments were going up the quickest, wouldn't that be nice? It'd be like going to a horse race and being allowed to hold your bet until you saw which horse seemed to be winning, then betting on that one. And if that horse started getting

passed, you could take your money back and invest it in the newest fastest horse. This is *exactly* what we are going to do with our Early Retirement Fund.

There are a couple of websites that most people don't seem to know about that ranks which investments are moving up the fastest over different periods of time: one year, six months, three months, etc. Instead of trying to PREDICT which companies and stocks will do well, why not just WATCH and see which ones are ACTUALLY doing the best, and then invest in them? The experts are always trying to PREDICT which ten or twelve stocks will be a winner out of millions, and they are almost always wrong. Do you really think you can predict better than them? I can't. But I can cheat and see which ones ARE the biggest winners and jump on board.

I call this "As-Isness". Almost everyone I talk to wants to *predict* the next big stock. Or they want me to predict the next big stock. That is next to impossible. But it is very easy to simply follow the long-term leader. To figure out which investments are at the front of the race, especially over the long term, and invest with them as long as they are performing. To me, investing is like betting on the tide. I like to follow the tide of the market, and bet in the direction of that tide. Then I see which investments are at the top of the biggest waves, and invest in those. When the wave hits the shore, stops its forward motion and starts to recede outward, its time to get out and wait for the next big wave. When the entire tide changes direction, you ride the new direction, with new types of waves. Or you wait on the sidelines until the tide comes back in.

I can't overemphasize how much easier it is to bet on a winner *during* the race than it is to *predict the winner beforehand*. I hope I am getting across to you how important this is.

For my Early Retirement Fund, I tend to invest in ETFs, especially leveraged ETFs, and maybe an individual stock from time to time. We're going to go over that now.

ETFs

My favorite aggressive investments for the Early Retirement Fund are ETFs, but especially leveraged ETFs. This is the secret niche I have found. It is not unheard of, but most people have never been exposed to it, or have any idea how lucrative they can be.

Leveraged ETFs is also an area that I received a lot of criticism from in earlier versions of my book- mostly from mainstream, academic investors. I'll address their concerns in a minute, but first let's go over exactly what an ETF is.

An ETF is an Exchange Traded Fund. They are like Mutual Funds in that they are a group of investments instead of one stock, but they don't have the fees or restrictions that Mutual Funds usually have. I prefer ETFs to individual stocks. They are safer and usually more predictable. If I ever refer to an ETF as an Electronically Traded Fund instead of an Exchange Traded Fund, please try to ignore it. I am a doctor and insurance companies are beginning to pay us with EFTs (Electronic Fund Tranfers). Sometimes I accidentally get my verbage backwards when talking about the two different entities- ETFs (Exchange Traded Funds) and EFTs (Electronic Fund Transfers).

There are ETFs made to mimic the S&P 500, the Dow Jones Industrial Average, the Nasdaq, the markets of other nations, the Gold Market, the Silver Market, and just about anything else you can think of. There are ETFs that make money when the market is going up, and there are ETFs that make money when the market is going down. Unlike Mutual Funds, you can buy and sell ETFs as easily as you can a stock or bond. The creation of ETFs was good enough to make me happy, but then the powers that be did something I really like- they created Double and Triple Leveraged ETFs.

A leveraged ETF is an ETF that is "leveraged"- it goes up and down faster than the basic ETF. A basic S&P 500 ETF for example, might go up 10% per year on average. But its double leveraged cousin goes up twice as fast, or 20% per year. Its triple leveraged cousin goes up three times as fast, or 30% per year. In 2014, TQQQ, which is a triple leveraged Nasdaq ETF, went up around 70%! Of course, leveraged ETFs go down faster too, so you have to know when to get off the elevator. We'll be going over that shortly.

Leveraged ETFs are able to increase price movement so drastically by using financial derivatives and debt to amplify returns. If that sounds complicated, it is. Some people believe that you shouldn't invest in anything you don't understand. I agree to a certain degree. If someone wants me to invest in land that I've never seen, I don't know the person or understand the deal- no way I'm going to do it. However, in the market, I don't need to understand every detail of every company or investment I invest in. I really only want to know if it is safe (not an unregulated investment that might go out of business) and if it is going up in a way I can capitalize and make money on. Fundamental investors will disagree with me. That is ok. I have respect for fundamentalists, I simply have my own way of doing things. I made about 12% on LUV (Southwest Airlines) in about a month's time not too long ago, yet I know nothing about the company or airlines in general. I made a really good return on a Latin America ETF a few years back, I think it was around 30 or 40%, yet I know nothing at all about their economy.

The speed to which Leveraged ETFs go up and down is the main reason for the criticism I received in earlier books on this investing method. And there is truth to it. Mainstream investment wisdom considers Leveraged ETFs to be dangerous and not at all for the beginner. Even the mainstreamers are beginning to change their tune about Leveraged ETFs, but it is true that Leveraged ETFs move FAST. If you are a beginner, I can't emphasize enough how aggressive Leveraged ETFs are. Please papertrade first, then invest in regular ETFs, and once you feel comfortable you can start investing in Leveraged ETFs.

I started out investing in Commodities. You buy Commodities on Margin. Margin is where you pay just a fraction of the money down to own something much more expensive. For example, say you buy a house for $100,000 but you only have to put down

$1,000 up front. If the value of your house goes up to $110,000 and you sell it, you just used $1,000 to make $10,000. This sounds great, and it is, as long as you MADE money, but the reverse is also true. What if you had put down that same $1,000 for the house, but instead of going up the value of your house dropped to $90,000. You just put in $1,000 and the value went down $10,000. If you had to sell the house you lost more than what you actually put in. This is where the term Leverage comes from. You are putting a fraction of money down, but making (or losing) the return on an object as if you had bought the entire object. You are "leveraging" your money.

This is the way of things in the commodity market- you put down a small amount of money to control a much larger item. Let's say you pay $1,000 to control $10,000 in cotton. What happens is you pay the $1,000, and basically borrow the rest of the money from the brokerage firm. If the price of cotton goes up from $10,000 to $12,000 and you sell, you just made fast money, and a lot of it compared to what you put in. This is leverage. This is buying on margin. You put in a fraction of the total cost of the object but made the full return. You put in $1,000 to make $2,000. In reality, you put in $10,000 and made $2,000, but because you only had to put in $1,000 to control the $10,000 position, your percent return was huge. Making $2,000 off of $10,000 is a 20% return on your money. But making $2,000 from $1,000, that is a 200% return.

But if the price drops $2,000, you just lost *more than you put in*. You only put in $1,000, but lost $2,000. When or if this happens, the brokerage firm would do a "Margin Call", basically telling you that the $1,000 you put in has been used up and you need to pay more. Many times, the people in the commodity market that killed themselves in the past were for this reason- you can lose much more than what you put in. Many people got too risky and bought as much commodity futures as they had money for. Let's say they had $100,000 to spend. They invested it all. But if the market dropped a good amount, they may have owed $500,000 on Margin Calls. It can be tragic.

This is why I switched to stocks. You cannot lose more money than you put in with stocks. You are not buying on margin with stocks. For me, the stock market is MUCH slower paced and easier on the emotions than the commodity market. You tend to make slower returns, but the much slower pace is easier to deal with.

The reason I like Leveraged ETFs so much is that you get much faster movements than with regular stocks or ETFs, somewhat close to the fast movement of a commodity, but it is still quite a bit calmer and you are not buying on margin. Your results are amplified, similar to a commodity, but you cannot lose more than you put in. And if you do like me, and get out if the investment turns down, you cut your losses short and ride your winners. As long as you do as I recommended, you are only investing excess money in these ETFs, not your regular Retirement Fund.

Overall, Leveraged ETFs have done me well. I like them very much. But again, if you are new, wade into them. Paper trade first, then do regular ETFs or a few stocks, and then work your way slowly into Leveraged ETFs. When you do get to Leveraged ETFs, start with Double Leveraged ETFs before you try Triple Leveraged ETFs.

I think that the mainstream investors invest so conservatively that using Leveraged ETFs scare them silly. Because I had started in commodities and was used to much scarier alternatives, Leveraged ETFs just don't bother me much at all. Compared to the commodity market I was used to, Leveraged ETFs are fairly mild and straightforward.

Here is the web address to the top rankings of the best performing ETFs:
http://etfdb.com/etfdb-category/leveraged-equities/?q%5Bs%5D=fiftytwo_week_return+desc#returns

And here is a screen shot as of 2/18/2015:

Symbol	Name	1 Week	4 Week	YTD	1 Year ▼	3 Year
INDL	Daily India Bull 2x Shares	+8.74%	+0.12%	+29.56%	+126.31%	-20.36%
RETL	Daily Retail Bull 3x Shares	+1.43%	+25.65%	+17.59%	+88.22%	+431.72%
SOXL	Daily Semiconductor Bull 3x Shares	+7.06%	+11.87%	+6.81%	+83.11%	+237.54%
CURE	Daily Healthcare Bull 3X Shares	+4.98%	+3.06%	+11.87%	+71.94%	+615.36%
USD	Ultra Semiconductors	+5.18%	+2.66%	+1.48%	+71.19%	+118.37%
YINN	Daily China Bull 3x Shares	+6.87%	-1.09%	-8.70%	+63.94%	+53.09%
TECL	Daily Technology Bull 3x Shares	+6.73%	+14.02%	+8.68%	+62.54%	+177.43%
TQQQ	UltraPro QQQ	+6.85%	+14.70%	+10.43%	+62.45%	+334.50%
UPRO	UltraPro S&P 500	+4.62%	+10.09%	-5.59%	+48.16%	+266.29%
SPXL	Daily S&P 500 Bull 3x Shares	+4.66%	+10.09%	+5.75%	+47.92%	+254.59%
XPP	Ultra FTSE/Xinhua China 25	+4.66%	-0.38%	+6.48%	+47.67%	+22.64%
RXL	Ultra Health Care	+3.47%	+2.73%	+8.69%	+46.53%	+301.12%
BIB	Ultra Nasdaq Biotechnology	+7.65%	+6.31%	+18.73%	+44.91%	+555.19%
FAS	Daily Financial Bull 3X Shares	+2.94%	+11.98%	-1.65%	+42.52%	+308.39%
UDOW	UltraPro Dow30	+3.00%	+8.24%	+3.24%	+41.09%	+182.85%
QLD	Ultra QQQ	+4.54%	+9.77%	+7.28%	+40.96%	+181.60%
FINU	UltraPro Financials	+2.26%	+11.56%	-3.53%	+40.56%	n/a
ROM	Ultra Technology	+5.74%	+11.29%	+6.20%	+40.33%	+110.49%

These are the fastest rising leveraged ETFs at the moment- the fastest horses in the race. I tend to start out looking at the 1-year return first and go from there. Which ETF has a really good one-year return, but also has a good three-year return, indicating that it is a good longer-term investment? There are several of them to choose from. Notice that the first one, INDL, is the highest ranked over one year, but its three-year numbers are pitiful. I wouldn't choose that one. Number two, RETL, looks much better. An 88% return for one year, and a 432% return for three years. That's some serious money growth!

To put this in perspective, remember that the stock market, and most financial and brokerage firms, average 10% per year. If you put ten thousand dollars into the average market, in three years it would basically be up thirty-percent, or three thousand dollars, bringing your total to thirteen thousand. But if you had put that same ten thousand into CURE above, it would have generated over six hundred percent, or sixty thousand dollars, over a three-year period, bringing your total to seventy thousand dollars!! See why I love leveraged ETFs? This is an extreme example, but you get the idea.

Before we go on, there is one more thing I need to mention. Those investments in the chart above that say "Bull 3x" means that they are triple leveraged and make their money when the market goes up- a Bull market is an up market. If you ever see investments that say "Bear" or "Short" or "Inverse", it means they make their money when the market goes down. A "Bear" market is a down market. I don't really like to invest in these. Never say never, but when the market goes down, it tends to do it very fast and very erratically. In theory, this can make you a lot of money. But in my experience, it is a very hard wave to ride. When I have lost money in the past, it is usually from trying to ride the "Bear" or "Short investments". I may change my mind in the future if I figure something out, but for now my advice is to not invest in Bear or Short investments. Instead, during Bear Markets, when the Tide is going out, I prefer to park my Early Retirement Fund money in REM, if it is doing well enough, and make lots of dividends. Also, when the market goes down, some sectors, like Gold and Silver tend to go up. I also look for those.

There are some people who claim to make a lot of money in Short Funds. They may. I simply haven't done well with them so my only advise right now is to avoid them. If you find someone that does well with them, you might be able to add them to your portfolio in down markets. I may even do it in the future. Who knows. But for now I still avoid them.

To the Charts

The next step is to look at the charts for the above symbols that look most promising. Let's look at the charts for RETL, SOXL, CURE, TQQQ, UPRO and SPXL. Why did I choose those? They are ETFs in the top ten of the race this year, who also have really good three-year stats. When I am looking at charts I am looking for a smooth upward growth, as opposed to a choppy up and down stock chart. I want smooth sailing, not choppy waters. I prefer the charts from www.StockCharts.com, and I usually look at as long term a chart as I can when picking an ETF- at least a five-year chart. Once I find a good one, then I'll take a closer look- usually a six-month to a year chart.

This brings up a point- on TV the "experts" and the news only show you very short term charts. Don't let those short term charts get you worked up. We are not day trading. Short-term charts are more "sensational looking", and the media wants you worked up. Don't let them get you there. You need to be calm and clear-headed to invest correctly.

Let's look at RETL first. If it is a good, smooth, upward chart, I'd jump right on it. It has a 432% return for three years, and is number two for the one year return, meaning it is still going strong. Here it is:

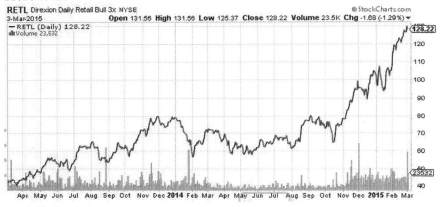

Chart courtesy of StockCharts.com

Well, it's a little choppier than I was hoping for, especially that hump around the 60-80 dollar range. It doesn't look as reliable as I would like. Let's look at the next ETF…

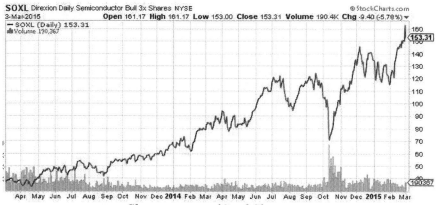

Chart courtesy of StockCharts.com

OK. I don't like how choppy SOXL is at all. I like RETL better. Remember, when the numbers go up and down a lot, it is very hard to know whether to stay in or get out. Especially when you are in Leveraged ETFs that have accelerated gains and losses. You would be a nervous wreck being in an investment whose price is fluctuating this much.

Lets go on to CURE.

Chart courtesy of StockCharts.com

Now that's more like it. Look at how much smoother the chart is. CURE has the first nice, smooth chart, of the top ten ETFs for the year. It is ranked fourth for the year, and is up 615% for the three-year term. Nice! So far this one is my favorite.

Let's go on to TQQQ:

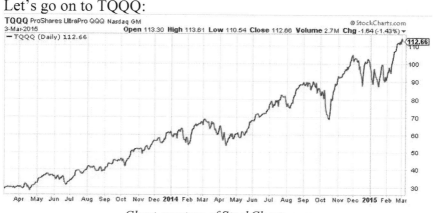

Chart courtesy of StockCharts.com

That looks doable as well. It's ranked eighth for the year, and has a 334% three-year return. I'd say it runs second to CURE so far.

Now for the last two:

Chart courtesy of StockCharts.com

Chart courtesy of StockCharts.com

Both of those charts look nice and smooth as well. However, they rank ninth and tenth for the year behind CURE and TQQQ, and their three year is in the 200% range compared to TQQQ's 300% range, which is behind CURE's 600% range.

Overall, I'd have to say that I would go with CURE. It is the highest one-year ranking chart that looks pretty smooth, AND its three-year return is 615%, the highest in the group of smooth charts by far.

Notice that all the charts have the same basic upward trend- they all look very similar. But some of the ETFs move up faster than others. And some do it smoother than others. We are simply trying to find the fastest and smoothest ride of the group.

TO SUMMARIZE:
1. **Step one** is to look at the top-ten ranking ETFs for the year. Also notice the other time frames, especially the three-year return.
2. **Step two** is to look at the charts, and find the ETF closest to the top of the year with the best one and three year returns that also has a good, smooth chart.
3. **Step three** is to buy that ETF. You basically take however much money you want to invest and divide it by the current price of the ETF. Let's say you are buying CURE, and you have $10,000. CURE is selling at $144.01 per share. $10,000 divided by $144 means you can buy around 69 shares. Remember that Scottrade will charge you $7 when you buy and $7 when you sell. This is not PER share, it is PER time you place a trade, no matter how big or small the trade is.
4. **Step four** is to put your investment information in your free Yahoo portfolio so you can keep up with it. Scottrade also keeps up with it if you don't want to mess with the Yahoo portfolio, but I find it easier to read and understand the Yahoo portfolio.
5. **Step five** is to monitor your investment about once per week. That is usually all you need.

** One more thing. The top ETFs are usually leveraged ETFs. "Leveraged" ETFs go up much faster than regular ETFs. They also go down much faster. If you don't have the "nerves" in the beginning for sitting out the dips when they occur, you should paper trade first (that chapter is coming up), then start investing in Non-Leveraged ETFs until you get comfortable. Once you get comfortable you can move up to Double Leveraged ETFs (2x), then eventually Triple Leveraged ETFs (3x).

You can choose Non-Leveraged, Double Leveraged and Triple Leveraged Rankings here:
http://etfdb.com/screener/#tableTab=returns

On this page, under filters, there is a category labeled Leveraged. Just choose Any, 3x, 2x or None. Choosing none will only rank the fastest rising non-leveraged ETFs for you.

If you want more help on this subject, go to the members area on www.MatthewBarnes-101.com and watch video tutorial number seven. Again, the password is QUAN

INDIVIDUAL STOCKS

I tend to prefer ETFs (especially Leveraged ETFs) for my Accelerated / Early Retirement Investment Fund. I don't completely avoid stocks, I just prefer ETFs when I can get them. Individual stocks can drop very dramatically. They can go out of business. They can go through mergers. ETFs, being made up of a large number of stocks and bonds and such, all in one entity, are much safer. If an individual stock or two in an ETF fund goes haywire, it usually doesn't affect the ETF all that much. This is comforting. And the Leveraged ETFs move up almost as fast as the best individual stocks do, but without the risk of it going out of business.

On occasion, when there is nothing performing well in the ETF world, or if I just want a change, or if there is a stock doing unusually well, I may invest in an individual stock. But I don't typically seek this out. I usually stick with leveraged ETFs whenever possible. However, I have made quite a bit on individual stocks in the past. When I do invest in an individual stock, I ONLY invest in those that are listed on the Dow, Nasdaq or the S&P 500. These are the safest, sturdiest stocks. These are reliable companies that I feel safe with. If they aren't on the Dow, Nasdaq or the S&P, I just don't trust them.

When I invest in an individual stock, I go through the exact same steps as when I invest in leveraged ETFs- I look for and invest only in "All Star" stocks. I get on the fastest rising elevator, follow it up for as long as it is going up, and then get off if it stalls or starts going down.

Here is the web address to the top rankings of the best performing individual stocks:
http://www.finviz.com/screener.ashx?v=141&f=idx_sp500&o=-perf52w

And here is a screen shot as of 2/20/2015:

No.	Ticker	Perf Week	Perf Month	Perf Quart	Perf Half	▼ Perf Year
1	LUV	2.94%	7.05%	13.05%	42.02%	107.89%
2	EA	2.62%	19.97%	34.52%	53.54%	107.52%
3	HSP	0.22%	36.93%	46.58%	59.42%	99.05%
4	EW	1.60%	4.33%	5.15%	37.81%	97.44%
5	AVGO	2.15%	6.34%	23.03%	47.78%	92.91%
6	FTR	-0.84%	22.24%	22.78%	29.49%	87.78%
7	KR	0.47%	8.92%	24.70%	44.88%	87.65%
8	AGN	2.80%	5.53%	9.69%	43.51%	84.16%
9	TSO	11.25%	22.27%	24.63%	41.22%	83.25%
10	LB	-2.08%	12.80%	20.58%	48.05%	76.89%
11	AAPL	2.40%	18.67%	12.58%	29.83%	73.89%
12	ANTM	1.82%	3.52%	12.43%	28.79%	67.50%
13	MO	0.13%	2.47%	14.05%	33.90%	63.99%
14	MNST	1.46%	2.29%	10.49%	37.03%	62.33%
15	MAR	5.04%	8.84%	7.88%	21.42%	62.20%

As you can see, I have not found a way to compare a three-year percent growth on these stock rankings as we did with the ETFs. A one-year will have to do for now. That is OK. Individual stocks don't usually keep rising forever like the overall stock market does. The overall market has some pretty big dips here and there, but overall it has always been in a steady upward climb. Individual stocks tend to have their day in the sunshine and then fizzle out and drop.

ETFs that mimic the overall market historically just keep going up. They do have their dips, but overall they keep going up. That's why I like leveraged ETFs. Overall, you know the S&P, Dow or Nasdaq ETFs, despite dips here and there, are continually rising, so they are a good bet. If you bet up, you will most likely be right overall. Individual stocks…not so much.

Now that we know the fastest rising stocks currently, lets look at their charts and see if any are going up smoothly. The bottom line is that the highest ranked stock with a smooth chart wins. Let's look at graphs of the first seven. I don't usually look much past the top seven to ten. LUV is the number one ranked stocked. Let's look at its chart:

Chart courtesy of StockCharts.com

We might have a winner right off. LUV's performance for the past year has been right at 108%. Its graph is pretty smooth, and in a predictable, uninterrupted up-trend. Unless another stock comes along that blows me away, I'm going to say that LUV takes the cake.

Next is EA:

Chart courtesy of StockCharts.com

EA is much choppier than LUV. It has gone up right at 108% in the past year, like LUV, but its chart is much more unpredictable.

Now let's look at HSP:

Chart courtesy of StockCharts.com

This chart makes me nervous. Why? Look how fast it is rising now. Whenever you see a stock price moving pretty much straight up, watch out. What goes up fast comes down faster. I may be wrong about this one, but better safe than sorry. This is the kind of chart that gets you greedy, and then the bottom drops out. I would much rather have a slower, smoothly rising stock like LUV, which is definitely still in the lead. Notice that around the $40-$45 price range there was a lot of "resistance". This means that the stock had a hard time moving out of that price range.

Fundamentalists point out that there is nothing wrong with HSP, that there was internal news that made the price jump, nothing to be afraid of. But in my experience, when things move "too far too fast", it is just best to avoid them. Along with "Inverse", "Bear" or "Short" funds, these type of charts are where I have lost the most money in the past. Again, I am more of a technical trader. It works for me so I use it. Fundamentalists watch for news and try to invest ahead of news they think would benefit the stock. In this case, a Fundamental investor that had invested in this company ahead of the news they felt caused the stock to rise would have done very well.

The stock market in general, and each stock you see, is, in my opinion, a direct measure of how optimistic or pessimistic the American people are at the moment. The more optimistic people are, the quicker and smoother the market moves up. The more pessimistic we are, the quicker the market drops.

This goes for individual companies too. The more optimistic we are about a company, the better its stock does. The more pessimistic we are, the worse it does. In the above graph, where the chart had resistance around $40-$45 per share, the chart is telling you that people were optimistic about the worth of the company until it got to around $45 per share. Then people became undecided, wondering if the company was really worth that much. When this happened the stock stalled.

If the people had become pessimistic, the stock would have dropped. But the people evidently decided the company *was* worth $45 or more, so optimism kicked in and the stock eventually "broke through" that resistance and then continued going up.

The same thing happens with the overall market. Un-decidedness causes the market to stall sideways, pessimism causes the market to drop, and optimism causes the market to rise. If most people are optimistic, but there is also some pessimism, the market rises, but looks choppy. If there is some optimism but there are a lot of undecided people, the market rises slowly. Want to see the optimism or pessimism of America, just look at a long-term graph of the Dow or S&P 500.

On to the next stock: EW

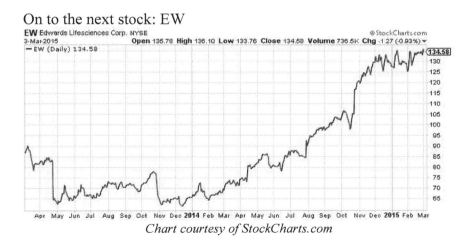

Chart courtesy of StockCharts.com

I don't like this one either. It's just too choppy. Not predicable enough for me. LUV is still number one. It is at the top of the list, and its graph is pretty smooth and easy to follow. This one's is not.

Now for AVGO:

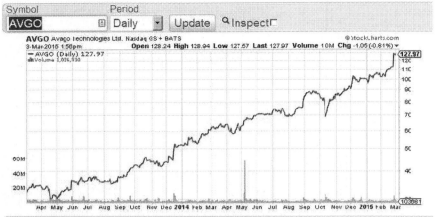

Chart courtesy of StockCharts.com

Now this one I like. Pretty predictable up trend, there are a dip or two but nothing terrible. AVGO made 92% last year and is still rising. But it is in 5th place overall. Its chart and LUV's chart are very similar looking, but LUV is going up faster, so I am going to stick with LUV.

For the sake of being thorough, let's still go over the last two graphs. But unless something crazy occurs, LUV is my choice. Here is FTR:

Chart courtesy of StockCharts.com

Nope. Not even close. FTR may be at the beginning of a good long up-trend, but for now it is too choppy, too unpredictable, and it has a lot of resistance to break through at $9 and $14 to continue its upward climb. LUV is still the best.

One more, KR:

Chart courtesy of StockCharts.com

Very, very nice. I would choose this one over LUV if it weren't in 7th place. BUT, as smooth and quick as that graph is rising right now, I think I'll compare it to LUV a little closer. Over the past six months, LUV went up 42% and KR went up 48%. This means KR may be picking up speed on LUV. I think I would still choose LUV, but to be honest, either one would probably be a great investment.

Lets compare the two one last way. On www.StockCharts.com, you can overlap two different stocks to see which one is rising quicker and more smoothly. Let's do this with LUV and KR:

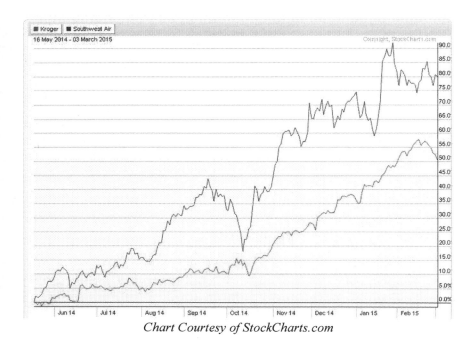

Chart Courtesy of StockCharts.com

The top line is LUV. The lower line is KR. LUV is definitely the winner. It is choppier than the very smooth KR, but it is also rising much faster. So LUV it is- or that's the one I would most likely choose.

TO SUMMARIZE: These are the same steps as when we were looking at investing in ETFs, only this time we are looking at stocks.

1. **Step one** is to look at the top ranking stocks for the year.
2. **Step two** is to look at the charts, and find the stock with the best one-year returns that also has a good, smooth chart.
3. **Step three** is to buy that stock. You basically take however much money you want to invest and divide it by the current price of the stock. Let's say you are buying LUV, and you have $10,000. LUV is selling at $44.78 per share right now. $10,000 divided by $44.78 means you can buy around 223 shares. Remember that Scottrade will charge you $7 when you buy and $7 when you sell. This is not PER share, it is PER time you place a trade, no matter how big or small the trade is.

4. **Step four** is to put your investment in your free Yahoo portfolio so you can keep up with it.
5. **Step five** is to monitor your investment about once per week. That is really all you need. We will go over how to know when the wave has fizzled and you need to get out in the next chapter.

If you want more help on this subject, go to the members area on www.MatthewBarnes-101.com and watch video tutorial number seven. Again, the password is QUAN

WHEN TO GET OFF THE ELEVATOR

Now that we have picked out an ETF (or a stock if you prefer), we need to know when to get in, and even more importantly, when to get out. This is where we need to talk about a moving average. The moving average line plots the AVERAGE price of the ETF or stock over a certain period of time. You can get 5 day moving averages, 15 day moving averages, 50 day moving averages, 200 day moving averages, and anything in between.

With StockCharts.com, Big Charts, and many other free charting sites, you can look at a price chart of your stock with different Exponential Moving Averages (EMAs) laid on top of your chart. What we are going to do is look at the price line on the ETF or stock we are in, and then overlap different moving averages over top of the stock price until we find one that "fits". It is easier to show you this than explain it, so we are going to use CURE and LUV, the ETF we liked best from the ETF list and the stock we liked best from the stock list.

First, let's talk about price lines. Here is LUV graphed with an Open, High, Low, Close line (OHLC):

Chart courtesy of StockCharts.com

This chart plots each day showing you a vertical line that represents all the prices from that day. The lowest point on each vertical line is that day's low. The highest point on that line is that day's high. The little dot on the left side of the vertical line is the opening price. The little dot on the right side of the vertical line is the closing price for that day. I don't tend to use this charting line, but a lot of people do, so I thought you needed to know how to read it. This is a three-month chart. I have been using a two-year chart but wanted a closer view for you to see the bars.

All the other charts I have been using have used "Closing" price displays. This is my favorite way. The closing price graph just plots where a stock price ends every day. The reason I like this type of chart is because it is a solid, single line, easy to read, and it tells you where the stock ended. To me, that's what really matters. Not how high or low a stock went during the day (for the most part), or where it started. Where it closed at tells me what people are really thinking about that investment. Whatever price the investment closes at is the true measure of how optimistic or pessimistic people are about that investment, for if that price made them uncomfortable they would have gotten out before the close.

Now lets take a Closing Price display chart of LUV and overlay a 50-day moving average:

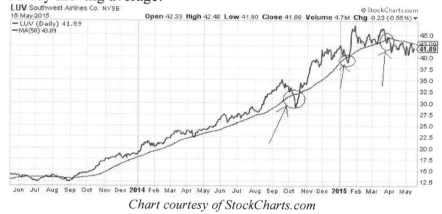

Chart courtesy of StockCharts.com

The upper line represents the closing price of LUV. The line below it represents the 50-day Exponential Moving Average. When the closing line of the stock dips down and breaks below the 50 day moving average, it is time to get out. Conversely, when the closing price breaks back up through the 50 day EMA, it's time to get back in. Note that the 50-day EMA fits LUV very well. You would have gotten out around $30, maybe again at $40, and definitely again around $43, and you'd still be out now, waiting for the price to break back above the moving average to get back in. I marked these areas with arrows. The first two breaks in the uptrend of LUV are both false alarms- but better safe than sorry. You never know when that dip will just keep going. The last dip LUV has taken is bigger, and probably means it is time to look for another investment.

* The IRS has a rule that if you lose money in an investment, then try to get back in that investment within 30 days, you get penalized. They don't care if you make money on an investment, get out, and then get back in- this makes them money. But if you lose money on an investment, they don't want you getting back in right away. Ask me how I figured this one out!

Next lets look at CURE, the ETF we chose from the top ETF list:

Chart courtesy of StockCharts.com

On this one, the 50-day EMA didn't fit so well. Notice that it was running too close to the closing price graph, so you ended up getting in and out needlessly over and over. Again, with the IRS ruling, you don't want to be getting in and out over and over and over. Instead, you want an EMA line that "fits" your investment so that it tells you when you really need to get out, but you don't end up with lots of false alarms.

Notice I have circled every place where the price line crossed the EMA line, indicating time to get in or out. You simply need to play with the EMA numbers until you find a "good fit" for that investment.

Here is CURE again, but with a 100 day EMA:

Chart courtesy of StockCharts.com

Now that is a MUCH better fit. You would only have gotten out once or twice on this one (notice the circled areas). Both times were still false alarms, but again, you never know when a big dip will just keep going. If you try an EMA that is too far away from the price line, trying to avoid all false alarms, you will end up losing too much of your profits when it really is time to get out.

This will be your EMA for CURE. You will watch its growth with the 100 day EMA imposed over it. Whenever CURE dips, you just want to make sure it doesn't dip under your EMA line. What this does is it gets you out of the market if things start to turn, but leaves you in until then. Are there ever false alarms? Yes. See the two circled areas above? But there's nothing you can do about that. Whenever a big dip occurs, you just don't know if it means the market is turning or not. So it is better to get out to be safe. You can get right back in (as long as you didn't lose money- the IRS rule) if it was a false alarm.

Here is an example of using the moving average to get in and out of an investment:

Chart courtesy of StockCharts.com

Notice that in this case the 100-day exponential moving average (EMA) fits the chart pretty well. The circles indicate where the price action crossed the moving average line. When the price line (the upper line) drops below the moving average line, it is time to get out. When the price line jumps above the moving average line, it is time to get in.

In the above chart, notice the large runs that you would have been in before the lines crossed and you would have gotten out. Notice also that there are times when the investment got choppy and would have gotten you in and out, over and over. This is why I like to find the fastest moving elevator, AND THEN get the smoothest chart. The smoother the chart, the less you have to worry about getting bumped around this way.

Still, it does happen from time to time. The best you can do is to cut the losers and let the winners ride. You will typically take small losses and big gains this way. But also remember the IRS rule. If you are in an investment and end up taking a small loss, you can't get back in that investment for at least 30 days.

Remember to use your EMA line as your flying instrument. Follow them when they tell you when to get in, and follow them when they tell you to get out. Most people, even if they know what they are doing, mess up because they get emotional. They might ride a great investment up, up, up. Then the investment fizzles, turns and starts to go down. Even though it's time to get out, they stay in hoping to make just a little more money. Then the investment starts to really drop. Now they have lost all the gains they made and are hanging onto the investment hoping it will go back up enough to break even. It doesn't. They finally get scared and sell out at a loss.

I know a guy who had profits of around $80,000 in a stock. He loved the stock. It had made him lots of money. But then the stock started falling. Instead of getting out like he should, he held on. He had grown *attached* to that investment. But that investment didn't care about him. When it fizzled and faded, it simply fizzled and faded. He ended up losing all but $5,000 of the gains he at one time had.

Don't do this. Get out when your instruments tell you to. I promise there will be another elevator to get on at some point; you don't have to hold on to the one you are on, no matter how good it has been for you.

Remember that you will lose small amounts from time to time. Remember that there will be years where the overall market is going down and that during these years it is a struggle to make money in anything. This is just normal. But you will typically make enough the rest of the time that it comes out in your favor in the end. You cut your losses on losers, and let the winners ride. We are all wrong from time to time. The market goes through cycles. Cut your loss and move on.

If you want more help on this subject, go to the members area on www.MatthewBarnes-101.com and watch video tutorial number eight. Again, the password is QUAN

PAPER TRADE FIRST

I've mentioned this many times, but if you are new to investing it really is best to "Paper Trade" first. Additionally, once you are secure paper trading, you need to "wade in" to real investing bit by bit. Maybe invest first in regular ETFs, and use very little money. Then maybe try a stock or two, as they tend to be a little more volatile than a regular ETF. Then work your way up to investing more and more money, as you feel comfortable. Eventually you may be comfortable enough for Leveraged ETFs, my favorite, and investing larger amounts. When you get to Leveraged ETFs, start with double leveraged before moving up to Triple Leveraged.

Back to paper trading. Let's say you decided that CURE is where you are going to invest your Early Retirement Fund Money. In order to paper trade, simply pretend that you bought some today. Use the actual amount of money you would be investing, figure out the number of shares you could buy, then "pretend buy". Put the number of stocks and what you paid for them into your free Yahoo portfolio as if you actually bought them.

Watch your portfolio at least once per week to make sure it is not doing anything crazy. Then go to StockCharts.com or BigCharts.com and look at the chart, again, just to make sure nothing crazy is going on. It literally takes me about three minutes, one day a week to look at my investments. When I get out of an investment, or when it is time to look for a new one, it takes me a bit longer, but that is rare. I get in and out of positions only a few times a year. So all in all I am running my "investment business" on just minutes per week.

There is also a website that offers a free paper-trading account. I wish there was such a thing when I was beginning- it is a very good idea, and so helpful.
Go to http://www.investopedia.com/simulator/ if you are interested (and I think you should) and open a free paper trading account.

As you get going, notice how much patience it takes to invest. You will probably look at your paper trade portfolio several times per day at first. You will most likely get frustrated because it goes down, or it is not moving up very fast. Watching your portfolio for growth is like watching your child grow. If you stare at your child every second of every day you will not notice how much he or she is growing, but people that only see your child once or twice a year will be astonished every time they see your child. Even if your investment grows 100% this year, and even if that growth was constantly up (which never happens) that means it will only grow around 8% per month, which is around 2% per week, which is around .4% per day (Monday through Friday). So if you are watching it close, it will look like a snail crawling.

Not only that, but 100% in a year is huge. Warren Buffett has been averaging, by my calculations, 30% per year the last few years. That comes to 2.5% per month, .625% per week and .125% per day (Monday through Friday). You will really go nuts watching that portfolio grow!

When the portfolio grows, it tends to go in spurts. So you will pull your hair out because the investment seems to be going nowhere. Then it will drop a bit. It will scare you. You will want out. Then when it does go up, it tends to go up a chunk and you get happy. But then it stalls again, or goes down again. Investing is a MENTAL game. You have to be mentally tough at first to be able to do it right.

Airline pilots are trained to look only at their instruments. Their instruments are always right. Sometimes things look weird when flying, or the pilots get disoriented. If they try to fly by human decision-making, it can mean their. So pilots are trained to trust their instruments no matter what. Only if the instruments fail are they to rely on their own decision making.

Investing is the same. We have a process. Find the best ETF or stock with the smoothest up-trending chart. Invest in it. Find the moving average that best fits the investment. Then use that moving average to make your decisions. If the stock stalls, or goes down a little, or the TV says your investment is worthless, or your neighbor says you're going to lose your farm, you have to have the mental fortitude to "trust your instruments". Be a machine. Don't go by instinct or a "feeling". Use your instruments. If the price action crosses the moving average indicating it is time to get out, then get out, NO MATTER WHAT. If the investment dips, but it did not cross your moving average, stay in NO MATTER WHAT.

Again, trading is mental. Having a system that works is only the beginning. Being mentally strong enough to hold the course and not let emotions take hold of you is the rest of the story. Ken Roberts, a famous commodity trader and teacher used to talk about this all the time. And I agree 100%. In addition, he recommended you read books that develop an Iron Will, your Emotional Muscles, so to speak, and so do I.

I am going to shamelessly plug another of my books right now. I hope you don't mind. I wrote a plain, modernized version of the ancient Chinese classic, The Tao Te Ching. The title of mine is called "The Wisdom and Peace of the Teachings of the Tao Te Ching" by Matthew Barnes. You can find it on Amazon, both in paperback and on Kindle. Of all the books I have read on being able to get into a "Zone", to get past the mental chatter, to keep those emotions in check, the Tao Te Ching is the one that did the most for me. This is why I created my own translation of it. If it does not do it for you, keep searching. The bottom line is that once you understand how this investment system works, you really do have to start working on yourself. You will be your biggest stumbling block.

In any event, the purpose of this chapter was to tell you to paper trade first. First of all, if you are new to investing, there is some experience you need to gain, some wrinkles you need to smooth out before you take your hard earned cash and put it into the market. You may think you understand things pretty well now, but I guarantee there are a few lessons waiting for you that only experience can provide.

The other reason to paper trade is to see how emotional investing can be. You need to pretend your own money is in the market, and watch how your emotions react to every fluctuation. When you can watch these fluctuations without letting your emotions get the best of you, without letting them take you over, so that your intellectual side can simply watch your instruments and make all your decisions based on the instruments, then you are ready for real money. But start small. Slowly increase how much you put in investments as you get mentally tougher and tougher. When you don't flinch at the fluctuations of your investment at the current level you have in, it is time to put more in. Eventually you will be all in.

Please do not rush this process though. This may be the most important chapter in the book. You have to be able to let your mind and emotions swing wherever they want, while you wait patiently behind the scenes, making the correct decisions logically, mechanically.

DON'T LISTEN TO THE NEWS, OR OTHER PEOPLE

Although you need to work on yourself so that you can make your decisions more logically and less emotionally, you still want to avoid, as much as possible, being exposed to things that affect you emotionally. No matter how good you get at controlling your emotions, too much exposure to emotion producing issues would affect just about anybody.

Here is a simple rule: don't watch the financial news and only tell like-minded and supportive people what you are doing. If you are in an investment and the "experts" on TV tell you your investment is terrible, it will eat on you. No matter how sure of yourself you are, you will still have that doubt at the back of your mind. At least until you get good at this system.

The "experts" don't bother me at all now, but they used to. In fact, the experts are usually telling people to get into investments I have already made money on and am getting out of. Several people I have tried to help invest along the way tend to not get in when I tell them to. They wait until the TV tells them to. Then, when I am close to getting out, the TV is finally saying to get in. When I get out, they again wait on the TV experts to agree. In the end, I usually make money doing it myself, and they typically lose money following the TV.

The other part of the rule is to not tell anybody what you are doing, aside from like-minded individuals. One issue I have with human nature is that everybody knows everything there is to know about everything, even if they know nothing at all. If you tell somebody you are controlling your own investments, they are going to start giving you all kinds of advice. Even if they have never invested a dime of their own money, they will feel it their duty to tell you what they think about your project. Much of the time it will be out of sincere concern, but this is a mental stress you don't need to expose yourself to. It can affect your ability to make good decisions.

"Be careful", "That's dangerous", "I think you should do this", "I don't think you should do that", "So and so on TV says your investment is a dud", and so on. They mean well, I think, but the bottom line is that everybody wants to give you advice. And they will hound you and make you want to tear your hair out. Even when you can tell them that you are doing very, very well, it won't matter. Even if you are beating the S&P average of 10% per year by a landslide, consistently, it won't matter.

Most people just cannot buck the system. The idea of doing their own thing and not following establishment's rules scare most people too much. The idea of you breaking the rules they live by also scares them to death for some reason. So be careful who you tell about your new venture. Even people that love you will drive you nuts. They are not trying to be mean, they honestly believe the TV over you. They are genuinely concerned for you. They don't and can't understand, and they think you are day trading or something crazy. They think this because the media teaches them this. You must do what the establishment says to do. 10% is all you can make. If you are bucking the system, you will lose. That is what the media has taught them, and they don't know any different.

Just avoid all this if you can. Trust me.

HOW MANY INVESTMENTS TO BE IN AT A TIME

What I'm about to say is controversial. Imagine that.

I don't believe, as I said earlier, in investing in a very wide variety of investments. In my opinion, the very wealthy tend to concentrate their wealth into just a few All Star investments. If you have 30 ETFs in your portfolio, it will water down the results you are going to get. The same goes with stocks. Instead, I like to keep things simple, and to BLITZ (concentrate all your forces on) the All Star, best performing investments.

Our first investment is in Berkshire Hathaway, which is Warren Buffett's company. Buffett is the Michael Jordan of investing. I think if any investment is safe, that one is. And his company tends to do better than the S&P 500 every year. In addition, his company is invested in about twelve other investments. So by investing in Buffett's company, we are actually invested in about twelve companies, which are being monitored and watched over by Buffett. If any of them were unsafe, Buffett would not have bought them. We are putting our Retirement Fund Money in here.

Our second possible investment is REM, a Real Estate Investment Trust or REIT. I typically only use this fund for my second, aggressive stock fund if the market is going down and there is no safe ETF or stock to get into. REM typically pays around 10% in dividends, which is great. And being a Trust, it is not one company, but like Berkshire Hathaway, is a conglomeration of a bunch of investments. Some of you may choose to get into REM so that all your Retirement Fund Money is not in one place. This is fine.

Lastly, we are mostly investing our Early Retirement Fund Money in an ETF or two. When we invest in ETFs, we are, once again, not investing in a single investment. ETFs are a bag made up of a slew of single stocks. If one of those stocks goes bad, it really doesn't affect the ETF much at all. From time to time I may invest in a single stock or two as well.

So, up to now, even though we are only investing in two or three investments really, those investments are actually made up of a bunch of other investments. So our investments actually ARE spread out already. Our investments are:

1. Berkshire Hathaway with our Retirement Fund Money (and maybe REM if you want)

2. The fastest rising ETF or stock with a good chart. I prefer ETFs. I usually aim at getting into only the best rising one, but sometimes if two or three investments are neck and neck I may split my money three ways and invest in them all.

* I may replace number 2 with REM if the market is going down and there is nothing good to get in, but only if REM's chart is looking ok. Like the other investments, REM is also a conglomeration of dozens of investments as well.

So how many investments should you invest in? I do as few as two and as many as maybe five or so at a time. But each of those investments are typically a bag of a bunch more. This is how I concentrate my investments on the best ones, but diversify my portfolio a bit as well.

Again, if there are two or three leveraged ETFs neck and neck, and all of their charts are smooth and nice, I may get in all three. If you bet on the top three racehorses, you can only win.

WHAT ABOUT OPTIONS?

Options are an investing strategy that is very different from the investing we are going over right now. Very different. It would take an entire other book just to explain options- how they work and the basic strategies.

If you want to branch out to options, have at it, but make sure you do your homework on them- take a few courses and paper trade them first before you jump in. www.Dough.com is the best resource I have found for learning to trade options. Check them out if you are interested- do all of their courses and take all of their quizzes and see what you think.

I know people I love and respect that are really into options, and that is great. I am starting to dabble in them myself. The upside is that if you do them right you can really increase your chances of success in growing money. The downside is that they do seem to take more time to analyze and keep up with (I am used to minutes per week), and they seem much less straightforward than what I am doing. That being said, some of the strategies are brilliant.

If you want to trade options, Scottrade and the other brokerages require much more information. You typically need an upgraded margin type account. They want to make sure you have enough experience and money to be playing with options. This says to me that options must be more risky for the average person than regular investing.

If you are a beginner and want to dabble in them, start with "Vertical Spreads". Again, look into these on www.dough.com. This is an option strategy that is fairly straight forward, low risk and with a high probability of success if you know what you are doing.

PROTECT YOUR GOLDEN EGG!

When you start building up a nice little nest egg, it is a really good idea to protect it. In this day and age, people love to sue for every little thing. If you are ever in a car wreck, or somebody slips and falls and gets hurts on your property, or something similar occurs, you want to make sure nobody can come after the nest egg you've worked so hard to build.

To do that, first obtain good insurance coverage on everything you have- your house, your car, everything. If you have good insurance and something bad happens you should be covered. If you have bare bones insurance and get sued, the other party may come after you for more than your policy will pay. And if the other party's lawyer finds out you have a nest egg, the lawyer and the other party may try to win the lottery off of you.

In addition to a good liability policy on your house and car, talk to your insurance agent about an umbrella policy to cover anything over what your regular policy will cover. Say your auto liability policy covers up to $1 million. If you are in an accident where someone dies, and you get sued for lets say $2 million, an umbrella policy will cover anything over the amount your regular policy is limited to.

The second thing you need to do to protect your money is to talk with an attorney or an accountant about setting up a trust to put your nest egg in so that others can't get to it. This is what the rich do. They put the bulk of their wealth into some kind of a trust so that most of their assets are not in their names. Instead, the bulk of their assets are in the name of their trust. A trust is basically considered a business that you are running. You might be the President, your spouse the Vice President and Secretary, etc. So if a person with most of their money in a Trust gets sued, the person suing can only go after things that are in the name of the person they are suing. Since the trust is considered a different entity than you, its assets are off limits.

When you need money to live on, you simply take a "draw" of however much you need at the time, and leave the rest in. It is basically just a slightly more complicated banking account that you store all your stuff in until you need it.

You don't want to put everything you own into the trust though. For example, if your car is owned by the trust and you get into an accident, the other person can sue the owner of the car, which is the trust. So instead, you want to own your house and car, etc, but keep your wealth protected separately in a trust.

Family Limited Partnerships (FLPs) are a good choice these days for the average person to protect their money in this way. An FLP is basically a business partnership type of trust fund. It is technically a business that you and your spouse manage together. You and your partner do not own the money in the FLP, the FLP does, but you and your partner manage it. Whenever you need money, you and your partner take out "partnership draws". By doing this, it places your nest egg out of reach if someone tries to sue you, yet you still have full access to it.

There are a few rules to follow with all Trusts to make them protect you like they should. Make sure you ask your lawyer or accountant what the rules are and follow them to a T. The rules are not many and they are not hard, but if you violate them, the Trust won't protect your money, as it should.

Once you have an FLP, you can tell Scottrade and they will transfer the name of the account from your name to the name of your Family Limited Partnership, thus putting your Scottrade account out of reach of predators.

KEEP UP WITH YOUR PROGRESS

For those of you that are like me and really like to keep up with everything, you are going to want to keep up with your returns to see what percent you are making with your money. Personally, every year, I keep up with the percent return I made and I compare it to the percent return of the Dow Jones Industrial Average, the S&P 500 and the Nasdaq for that year.

For a simple method of keeping track of your returns, simply write down how much money you have in your Scottrade account on January 1st of the current year. Then on December 31st write down how much you have now. The difference is your total fund growth for the year.

Here is an example:

Balance on January 1st	$10,000
- Balance on December 31st	- $12,000
= Total Investment Fund Growth	= $2,000

Now to get your percent growth for the year:

Total Growth / Starting Balance	$2,000/$10,000 = .2
	.2 x 100 = 20%

So that gives you your total growth for the year of $2,000, which comes to 20%. The only problem is that includes the amount of money you put into your Retirement and Early Retirement Funds over the course of the year. To correct for that:

Balance on January 1st:	$10,000
- Balance on December 31st	- $12,000
- Amount you added to the fund that year	- $500
= Investment Growth for the Year	= $1,500

Now to get your percent growth for the year of your investments alone:

Investment Growth / Starting Balance	$1,500 / $10,000 = .15
	.15 x 100 = 15%

Now you know how much your overall investment fund grew this year, including the money you added to the fund during the year: $2,000, which is 20%.

You now also know how much your investments grew on it's own: $1,500, which is 15%.

Look up how much the Dow, S&P and Nasdaq made that year and compare your 15% to it to see how well you are investing.

If you want more help on this subject, go to the members area on www.MatthewBarnes-101.com and watch video tutorial number ten. Again, the password is QUAN

A DREAM COME TRUE- LIVING OFF YOUR INVESTMENTS

We are on the last step. When you save up enough money to live off of your investments, let's say one million dollars, you need to know how much you can spend each year. You don't want to take more out of your investments than you are making in returns. The goal is to leave the original one million alone, and live only off the interest it is making for you. You want to live off your money generator, without hurting the generator itself; pluck leaves from your money tree, but leave the trunk and branches unscathed to grow more.

Let's say you have a million invested, and that it made you 10% last year:

Original Nest Egg Amount	1 million dollars
Interest Earned Last Year	10%, which is $100,000

You can spend UP TO however much interest you made last year. So in the above example, you can live off of UP TO $100,000 this year. No more. BUT, it is smarter to live off about 70% of the interest from the last year and leave the other 30% in. First, this allows our nest egg to keep growing a bit, even in retirement. But also, if you average 10% per year (we are hoping to do better than that, but let's use that as an example), then you are not making 10% *every* year; you are making that on AVERAGE. One year you might make 20% and the next 0% or even -5%. If you spend ALL the interest during the good years, you might not have any at all during the bad.

No matter how you decide to do it, never take out more than the interest from the year before. That would be like having a money tree making you $100,000 in leaves per year, but you get greedy and cut the tree down. You can either live off the leaves forever, or kill the tree and have a limited amount of money. Forever is smarter.

Once you decide how much money you are going to live on this year, do not take out all the money you need at once. Only take out what you need as you need it. If you made 10% last year, and that gave you $100,000 to live off this year, you are going to take out 70% and leave the rest in. That gives you $70,000 to live on for the year. $70,000 comes to a little more than $5,800 per month. Once per month, simply take out the $5,800 for that month.

If you took the full $70,000 at once for the whole year, then you would be removing that money from the safety of your trust for one thing. If you got sued, that $70,000 wouldn't be safe. Also, that money could still be earning interest until you need it. By only taking out what you need, when you need it, you are leaving whatever you can in to make you even more money until you need it. Even in retirement, you can let your nest egg grow so you can end up making even more interest, which means you have more money you can take home.

Two more things: First, you will be paying taxes on the money you remove from your investments. When you are ready to start living off your investments, sit down with your accountant or tax professional and have them help you estimate how much you need to put aside for taxes. You don't want to get in trouble with the IRS, or end up having to take a chunk out of your Money Generator to pay Uncle Sam for back-taxes.

Secondly, if this method of taking money out sounds too complicated, talk to a financial advisor about annuities or some other simple method of storing your nest egg. Say your goal is one million dollars. Once you have that nest egg, you could put the nest egg into an annuity or something similar. After you put your lump sum in, an annuity will pay you a certain amount for the rest of your life. This simplifies things greatly. You now just sit back and let them send you checks for the rest of your life.

A lot of people like annuities. A lot of people don't. There are high up front fees, but at the same time they are very convenient. If you are interested just talk to a financial advisor or accountant and see what you think.

I tend to avoid having someone manage my money when I'm trying to build wealth, but once it is built, I am in favor of storing it in something safe like an annuity. I would not, however, take my nest egg and let a financial advisor put that money back into the market. I have seen too many financial advisors lose people's nest eggs. Safe annuities? Yes. Let them invest your money? No.

WHAT ABOUT IRAs, 401Ks AND THINGS LIKE THAT?

I am not a big fan of IRAs and other government-backed entities like that. If you have one at work, no problem- use it. I would still do this investment system in addition to that one. I am self employed and had to figure out my own retirement plan. The one thing I found out about IRAs along the way is that I just don't like them. There are just too many rules, regulations and penalties.

I tried setting up a few of these entities at my work for my employees, my wife and I at one time. The rules and regulations were confusing, there were too many penalties if you needed your own money for an emergency, and somehow we were going to be putting far more into our employee's funds than into ours. There were also strict rules on what you could and could not invest in. The funds I invest in were not on the list. At all. Ever. Those that were on the list were pitiful producers compared to the returns I was used to.

I have a friend that retired and had to get a little money out of his retirement fund. He was told there were no penalty fees. After he took the money out he was hit with a BIG penalty. He asked if he could turn around and put the money back in as if he hadn't taken it out and get his penalty fee waved. He was told yes, if he returned the money the fees would be waived. He put his money back in. Not only did he not get the penalty fee back, but the advisor that did it for him got another cut of his money for putting it back into the investment. When he first invested the money the financial expert got a cut of the money, and that expert got another cut for putting the money back in. Nobody, even the financial experts in the know, seem to know how these things work, and take every advantage to make more in fees.

No, I prefer to keep my money simple and within reach. I know I might pay more taxes initially, but I'll take that over all the mess. It's ok if you disagree with me on this. Many people I respect and care about do. Learn about it and see what you think.

AFTER THE MORTGAGE AND/OR STUDENT LOANS ARE PAID OFF

Earlier, I mentioned not including your mortgage or student loans as debts to be paid off before you start investing. If you wait until those are paid off you might be 80 before you start saving and investing. For those debts, just make your regular payments for now.

If you get to the point where you have enough money in your investments to pay those off, and still are on schedule for retiring early and with enough money, it is ok to pay those off early.

If you just make your regular payment to these two debts, and end up paying one off before you retire, "Snowball" half of that money into paying off the other debt. In other words, if you are paying $1,000 per month to your mortgage and $1,000 a month to student loans, and you pay off your mortgage, take $500 of what was your mortgage payment and add it to your student loan payment of $1,000 making the total payment $1,500 per month. Let the other $500 "float" to pay your bills and end up making you more "Fun Money" and "Early Retirement Money". This way, you both accelerate becoming debt free, but you also reward yourself a bit.

Once both bills are paid off, "Snowball" half of the payment into your Retirement Fund or Early Retirement Fund and let the other half "float" like before. All investing and no Fun Money leads to a boring life. I don't understand the point in that. You should enjoy, but plan ahead as well. Split your money between the future and now. That's my opinion anyway.

SUMMARY AND ACTION STEPS

1. Start keeping up with your bills so that you know how much money you spend on necessities versus your income. The leftover money is Excess Money that is going to be split between Early Retirement Investments and having Fun.

2. Figure out how much money you will need to retire comfortably at the age of 65.

3. Open up a Scottrade Account, create a free Yahoo account, set up a free portfolio and set up a free www.BigCharts.com or www.StockCharts.com account.

4. Start putting your Retirement money into Berkshire Hathaway (BRKB). You can split that with the Real Estate Investment Trust with the symbol REM if you like.

5. Apply your Early Retirement Fund Money to paying off credit cards and other debt (not mortgages or student loans) first.

6. After the debts are paid off, funnel your Early Retirement Money into building up an adequate savings.

7. Once the debts are paid and you have a good savings account, start investing your Early Retirement Fund Money, but paper trade first. When you are comfortable, start with real money, but start off with small amounts in case you aren't as up to speed as you think you are.
   a. Invest in the fastest rising Stock All-Stars, or
   b. The fastest rising ETF All Stars. I choose ETFs.

8. Protect your money as it starts to grow with good insurance and some sort of a trust fund.

9. Keep up with how fast your money is growing and compare it to the Dow, the S&P and the Nasdaq to make sure you are doing as well as you should.

10. When you can live off the interest on your investments, do. And if you keep working, simply put all the money you make into your investments.

Now you are earning your money once and spending it all forever!! You will never earn and then spend another dollar. You may earn more money, but you will never spend it. You will only spend its children.

VIDEO TUTORIAL WALKTHROUGHS

Some people need to see things done, and not just read about them.

As I mentioned earlier, I have set up a website to help those who need more than instructions from a book. On the website are video instructions of all the steps we have gone through for those of you that need to see these things done visually. Like the book, the videos will be short and to the point. I have also added a few spreadsheets to the members area that you can download to help make the calculations we go over in this book

The videos and spreadsheets will be found under the Members Only pull down under the Investing tab on my website, www.MatthewBarnes-101.com. As buyers of this book, I consider you Members. The password for "101" is QUAN. All caps.

I have also set up a newsletter, "The Money Club", to go with the book and the video tutorials. I hold nothing back in this book. If you read the book and follow the instructions you don't need me. Especially if you also follow the video tutorials. You can do the same thing I am doing and get the same results. It is a skill though, and it does take time to really get a handle on.

If you do want more help, that is what the newsletter is for. You can start learning this system correctly, right off the bat, skipping much of the learning curve.

The newsletter is not free, but it is very reasonably priced, especially considering the information you are receiving. I am opting to having a lot of members who pay a small monthly fee instead of charging a lot and only having a few people being able to afford it. You can cancel any time if you don't think the newsletter is for you.

Again, here is the website: www.MatthewBarnes-101.com
If you want more information on my system, including The Money Club newsletter, go to the bottom of any page on my website and enter your email address.

FURTHER RESOURCES

I know this information can be a little overwhelming if you are a beginner, even a simplified version like my system. I have been reading books on money management and wealth building since I entered the workplace years ago- I knew early on I wanted to be free of the tyranny of money. Along the way there were several books and systems of managing money and ways of investing that resonated with me and helped shape the system I now use. I'd like to recommend a few to you.

The first is *Rich Dad, Poor Dad* by Robert Kiyosaki. This book goes very deeply into the idea of using the money you earn to buy a money generator instead of spending it all. I highly recommend this book for a deeper understanding of this concept.

The second is *Financial Peace* by Dave Ramsey. Many of you have probably heard of this book. Ramsey introduced me to the idea of compartmentalizing money. I don't do it quite the same way as he taught, but my system of money management was influenced greatly by his.

If It Doesn't Go Up Don't Buy It by Al Thomas, *How to Make the Stock Market Make Money for You* by Ted Warren, the works of Ken Roberts, *How I made $2,000,000 in the Stock Market* by Nicolas Darvas, and the works of Burton H. Pugh are the books that most influenced the system I use now for investing. I do not quite do what they taught, but their unique ways of looking at investing got me to where my investing is today. Each of these teachers developed a unique, non-mainstream approach to investing, and as a result, made a lot more money than the "experts" that followed establishment rules. I very much appreciate these innovators' ability to break from the norm and pioneer a new way. I am now coming to realize just how much gumption it takes to do such a thing.

Lastly I'm going to recommend my own book, *The Wisdom and Peace of the Teachings of the Tao Te Ching*. Years of study (and a lot of trial and error) has shown me that investing on your own requires the ability to stay calm and focused, and to have the nerve and will-power to ride the waves of the market. The Tao Te Ching, more so than any other book out there, has helped me to do that most successfully. Investing is 50% knowing what to do and 50% doing it. This may sound easy, but when emotions get going, it is hard to follow even the simplest of plans. Developing an iron will plus the ability to remain calm within the eye of the hurricane while life violently spins around you not only helps with investing, but with life.

BIO

Matthew Barnes is an avid learner who spent his early years in North Carolina. He was born in Greenville, NC and has lived in New Bern, Roanoke Rapids, Henderson (where he spent most of his childhood) and Raleigh, where he attended the University of North Carolina State. After obtaining degrees in Biochemistry and Chemistry, he attended Chiropractic School in Marietta, Georgia, where he graduated third in his class. Since that time, he has studied acupuncture and Chinese medicine, and settled down in rural Tennessee with his wife, 3 cats, 4 dogs, a crazy mother-in-law and a partridge in a pear tree. He has been in Tennessee for over 20 years now.

His main interests are learning, exploring, exercising and writing. Most of his works so far have been on spiritual-type themes, though he has also written a book on self-investing- another one of his hobbies.

To check the progress on his other works, go to:
https://www.amazon.com/-/e/B00SDYKSZ2

*LETTER FROM THE AUTHOR

Dear Reader,

Thank you for reading my book! You've made my day ☺

I hope you enjoyed *Investing 101*. More than that- I hope that I have helped you to make your life better.

Positive feedback on Amazon can literally make or break a book. If you liked my book, please leave me a positive review on Amazon- five stars would be great if you don't mind. It does not need to be professional at all, one or two sentences is fine. For those of you that do leave feedback, please contact me and let me know so I can thank you personally. My personal email address is Dr.MatthewBarnes12@gmail.com.

Because the number of reviews and the number of stars awarded in those reviews can so strongly affect a book's success, I am asking that if you have input towards my book that is not so positive, please share it with me at Dr.MatthewBarnes12@gmail.com instead of giving my book a bad review on Amazon. I don't want a difference of opinion to leave a permanent scar on my rating.

I like receiving feedback that can help me find and correct errors. I am serious about trying to improve my book. On a deeper level though, not everyone that reads my book will see eye-to-eye with me. That doesn't mean we can't still be friendly towards each other.

If you have a difference of opinion with me, I'd like to hear it- as long as you are cordial, and as long as your opinion is based on actual experience, not theory. I am completely interested in any method of investing that equals or beats the markets or my results. However, I am not interested in the millions of theories out there that each person has, if they are not backed up by actual experience and tangible results.

My opinions on investing have be forged in the heat of battle. I have developed and molded them over time, learning from actual experiences I've had in the markets. I am still learning.

If there are mistakes I need to correct, or improvements that need to be made, I want to know about it. If you have discovered investing methods that are yielding great results, I want to hear about that too. But I don't have time to answer every email about how you disagree with my methods. Especially if you have never invested on your own.

Thank you for spending time with me!

Matthew Barnes